10 Essential Strategies

for *Improving* Student Achievement

James Harris, Ph.D

SCHOOL OF EDUCATION
CURRICULUM LABORATORY
UM-DEARBORN

ISBN: 0-9774033-0-0

Additional copies may be ordered from:
Amcan Publishing and Productions
P.O. Box 130
Saline, MI 48176
(toll-free) 866-405-1300
(fax) 734-429-1260
www.amcanpublishing.com

Book design and layout by Words Plus Design,
www.wordsplusdesign.com

Printed in the U.S.A.

Contents

Dedication

This book is dedicated to my parents, Rev. James Harris and Mrs. Emma Victoria Harris, and my brother, Henry Thomas Harris. Our family focus is always on the love of education as a fundamental part of life. Thanks to my parents for providing the best education possible to their two children.

About the Author

Dr. James Harris has become known nationally for his extensive work in the areas of school leadership, curriculum, school finance, and research in education. He earned degrees from Virginia State University and the University of Michigan. He earned post-doctoral certificates from the Kennedy School of Government at Harvard University.

The training that he received from these three great universities prepared him to serve as a teacher and administrator in Detroit, Michigan; high school principal in Joliet, Illinois; assistant superintendent in Aurora, Illinois; superintendent in North Chicago, Illinois; superintendent in Buffalo, New York; superintendent in Inglewood, California; and superintendent in Taylor, Michigan.

Under his leadership, many new and innovative programs were developed and implemented in various school districts. In Buffalo, he implemented the parent and school partnership program using the Epstein model from John Hopkins University. He organized the City Honors High School for academically gifted students in Inglewood, California. He fostered the involvement of parents as partners with the schools in all of his districts. Above all, he was innovative in improving student achievement in all of the districts that he led.

Dr. Harris is a futurist who believes that adults must be held responsible for creating schools for students to achieve at high levels. His philosophy of education is deeply rooted in the research of John Dewey, Ron Edmunds, Stephen Covey and Loraine Monroe. He believes that all children can learn when adults create the proper environment for learning.

Having served as an educational leader in many sections of the United States and Japan, Dr. Harris has amassed a wealth of experiences and methodologies for effective teaching, assessment, school leadership and parental involvement in schools. This book shares the depth of knowledge and practical experiences gained from his extensive professional life in the field of education.

INTRODUCTION

There is an ever-growing interest among many people about improving student achievement. Parents, school employees, politicians, and business persons are focusing time and resources on the central elements related to improving student achievement. The philosophical concept that all children can learn is beginning to take root in the American culture at a lightning rate.

Fortunately, the American culture is beginning to realize that it is in the best interest of the nation that focus be placed on improving the education of all young people. It is in our best interest that we educate, at a high level, all of our citizens in order to maintain our standard of living and our democratic values. It is clear to an ever-growing number of people that improving student achievement is the key to the growth and continuation of the American way of life. It is clear that many people are now realizing that our nation is truly the melting pot for the various races and ethnic groups from around the world. With such a variety of people living in our country, education seems to be the glue for keeping our principles of freedom in place.

Educationally, we have come a long distance in our country. Just think about it for a few moments. In the 1700s and 1800s in this country, formal education was organized primarily for the aristocrats. The founding fathers of the country, George Washington, Thomas Jefferson and others, worked to educate the elite and wealthy families. The concept of educating all children was not in vogue during the early years of our country. The "haves" were able to access educational opportunities. The "have- nots" were relegated to lives of manual labor, slavery, illiteracy, and limited opportunities for advancement. Improving student achievement for all students was only a fantasy of a concept yet to be brought to life in the form of the common school.

Placing things in perspective relative to improving student achievement, one can assume that the early days in America were characterized by people striving to survive. From Columbus's arrival to 1776, the country paid little attention to universal education for all because of a variety of factors. The Revolutionary and Civil Wars fought in this country consumed the attention of the leaders of the time. The westward expansion and the clearing and settling of land demanded that most young people spend time working, not sitting in schools. The early agrarian and settling period thus provided little time for focus on improving academic achievement for most young people.

The interesting history of education in America shows that the focus on education really began taking root during the late 1800s and 1900s. The 1800s witnessed the establishment of such great institutions as the University of Michigan, Harvard University, and Yale University. During that period, most states began establishing legislation for the organization of public schools. Farmers, business persons, churches, and other groups began organizing various schools to educate a larger number of young people. The interesting fact of the early days was that the concept of educating all children was not legally or politically considered. Thus, children from low socio-economic and minority strata were not given serious consideration for equal educa-

Introduction

tion. Educating larger numbers of children was not widespread, but that concept would take root and truly emerge over a period of 150 years.

From 1850 to 2001, the United States witnessed a remarkable number of events that gradually led to the focus on improving student achievement for all students. Following is a partial listing of some of the events that moved the country to truly focus on improving the education of all children:

- Emancipation Proclamation
- Ending of the Civil War
- Theoretical Research on Education by John Dewey
- *Brown v. the Board of Education,* 1954
- National Defense Act
- President Johnson's War on Poverty
- The Civil Rights Movement
- Goals 2000
- Publication of *A Nation At Risk*
- Governors' National Conference
- Standards in Education
- No Child Left Behind Act of 2001

In one way or another, all of the above influenced the actions and conscience of a large number of citizens relative to education. In the late 1900s, there were a massive number of research projects and pedagogical models that accelerated the process of educating children. All of the models professed the objective of improving student achievement. During the last 50 years of the 1900s, the plethora of concepts professing to improve student achievement included the following:

- Cooperative learning
- Cooperative teaching

- Cooperative discipline
- Looping
- Special Education
- Bell curve
- Inclusion of Special Education students in regular education classes
- Tracking
- Differentiation
- Direct instruction
- Ability grouping
- Focus on phonics
- Focus on Whole Language
- Authentic assessment
- Authentic teaching
- Hands-on learning
- Magnet schools
- Gifted programs
- Distance learning
- Home schooling
- Charter schools
- Theme schools
- J-curve
- Year-round school
- TESSA

The business and political segments of our country have gotten into education and have pressed strongly for improving student performance. Business persons have helped to usher into education business philosophies and models of operating. They have pressed for greater accountability and measurable objectives for education. Making test scores the bottom line has been the clarion call for the business-minded model. In business, measurable objectives are targeted with the expectation that everyone in an organization would work to meet the objectives. In sales, salespersons are expected to be creative in reaching their sales quotas; the alternative is hearing "You're fired." The Donald Trump business approach of achieving the objective without excuse or risking being fired, while popular in many circles, is being debated for its level of compatibility with the reality of factors in the field of education. Opponents of the business model creeping into the educational process often point to the fact that in business and manufacturing, the owners can order parts and components that have no defects. They can refuse to accept parts and components that do not meet their standards and specifications. In other words, they can send back materials that they deem in need of remediation. In public education, the schools have to accept, teach, and educate to high levels all students who enroll regardless of race, creed, gender, national origin, socio-economic background, and educational level. Public schools cannot send back those students who need remediation. Public schools take all children and teach them. The latter fact is often missed by some people.

Politicians, from the President of the United States to governors to mayors, are getting involved in the educational process at an ever-increasing rate. On the national scene, the No Child Left Behind Act (NCLB) of 2001 is being implemented across the country. Some citizens are excited about the long-term impact of the law in forcing schools across the country to improve student achievement. The law requires each state to develop measurable objectives and standards to be tested annually. The timeline in the law calls for 100 percent of students to perform at proficient levels by the year 2014 as determined by the individual states. Most states have established stratified benchmarks that increase periodically toward the 100 percent mark. For example, the State of Michigan has established the following benchmarks for schools to reach in order to show continuous progression toward the 100 percent mark:

Year	English Language Arts			Mathematics		
	Elem.	Middle	High	Elem.	Middle	High
2002	38%	31%	42%	47%	31%	33%
2003	38%	31%	42%	47%	31%	33%
2004	38%	31%	42%	47%	31%	33%
2005	49%	43%	52%	56%	43%	44%
2006	49%	43%	52%	56%	43%	44%
2007	49%	43%	52%	56%	43%	44%
2008	59%	54%	61%	64%	54%	56%
2009	59%	54%	61%	64%	54%	56%
2010	59%	54%	61%	64%	54%	56%
2011	69%	66%	71%	73%	66%	67%
2012	79%	77%	81%	82%	77%	78%
2013	90%	89%	90%	91%	89%	89%
2014	100%	100%	100%	100%	100%	100%

The required achievement percentage in the state is the same for all schools and districts (annual state objective). The bottom line is that the Michigan annual state objective in Language Arts and Mathematics will increase each year until it reaches 100 percent for all grades and all subjects in 2014 in order to meet the NCLB requirements.

The No Child Left Behind Act is being hailed by many people as the single most important piece of legislation impacting the concept of educating all children since the 1954 *Brown v. Board of Education*. The NCLB Act requires schools to communicate to the public the levels of achievement by students. The law also allows for parents the choice of moving their children from schools that are not performing at adequate levels. The law thus forces schools to improve student achievement or go out of operation. Is that good or bad policy? The law is being debated daily at all levels — nationally, statewide, and locally.

An interesting point put forth by some is that the NCLB Act is really an unfunded mandate that sounds good rhetorically but, in effect, lacks credibility and has little chance of success. This point of view is based on the fact that schools are being pressed to educate students at high levels, in many cases without the needed funds, personnel, and facilities, particularly in urban and rural areas. For example, in parts of California and Alaska, school officials have had difficult times recruiting and maintaining qualified teachers. Believe it or not, there is still a shortage of highly qualified teachers in certain parts of the country. In many urban areas, it is common for substitute teachers to work for many years teaching subjects that they know very little about. Some schools have to welcome the substitutes and teachers with weak training due to circumstances beyond their control: low salaries, poor working conditions, unsafe neighborhoods, dilapidated buildings, lack of supplies, unorganized curriculum, weak parental support, major student disciplinary problems, and many other factors. Practitioners in the education field are working to implement the law even though they know that the law is fraught with major imperfections. NCLB is now the law of the land in education. Until it is changed, those districts interested in accepting federal funds must comply with the tenets of the law.

It should be noted that many good things are emerging to foster improvements in student achievement based on NCLB. For example, most school districts are placing focused attention on the following:

• Curriculum writing
• Curriculum mapping

- Curriculum scope and sequencing
- Diagnostic testing
- Alignment of curriculum to state and national standards
- Disaggregation of data from student test scores
- Major staff development
- Extra time and extra help for students
- Pacing of instructing
- Upgrading of instructional materials aligned to standards
- Encouragement of all students to participate in the testing process
- Supplemental services
- Tutoring

NCLB might not be a panacea, but it is having an impact on student achievement.

Insights into the pedagogy of teaching show that many strategies and factors must be taken into consideration when working to improve student achievement. The factors go together and are not always in isolation. For example, it is very difficult to teach children who come to school hungry, abused, unloved by parents, and without necessary supplies. Thus, teachers have to cope with factors that require creativity and skillful use of the system for the good of students in order to teach. Pedagogical training helps in delivering the curriculum when a myriad of other factors work together in a positive manner.

After many years of research and practical experiences in the field of education, I have organized in this book the ten essential strategies for improving student achievement. When properly implemented, the ten strategies will foster schools and classrooms that are nurturing for students and high achieving. The ten strategies can serve as the bedrock for school districts and individual local schools that are dedicated to focusing on the achievement of children. Taken together, the strategies are supported by volumes of research from such notables as John Dewey, Stephen Covey, Ron Edmonds, Madeline Hunter, and many others.

It should be noted that special appreciation is expressed to Dr. Stephen Covey, author of *The 7 Habits of Highly Effective People*, for his impact on the professional life of this writer. As a high school principal at Joliet Central High School in Joliet, Illinois, I had the opportunity to attend a six-day workshop taught by Dr. Covey at the Sun Dance Center in the State of Utah. Even though the majority of the people in attendance at the workshop were corporate executives from Fortune 500 companies, as an educator, I was immersed in the following "7 Habits" taught by Dr. Covey — not to make more money, but to use the habits to improve student achievement:

- Be proactive
- Begin with the end in mind
- Put first things first
- Think win-win
- Seek first to understand then to be understood
- Synergize
- Sharpen the saw

My best to you as you read and immerse yourself in the ten essential strategies for improving student achievement based on research and proven practical experiences.

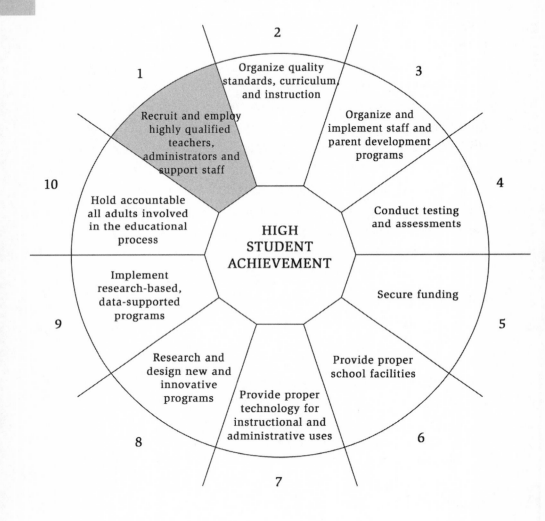

1. Recruit and employ highly qualified teachers, administrators and support staff

2. Organize quality standards, curriculum, and instruction

3. Organize and implement staff and parent development programs

4. Conduct testing and assessments

5. Secure funding

6. Provide proper school facilities

7. Provide proper technology for instructional and administrative uses

8. Research and design new and innovative programs

9. Implement research-based, data-supported programs

10. Hold accountable all adults involved in the educational process

HIGH STUDENT ACHIEVEMENT

Ten essential strategies for adults supporting high student achievement.

STRATEGY NUMBER ONE:

Recruit and Employ Highly Qualified
Teachers, Administrators and Support Staff

The old saying that "a chain is as good as its weakest link" rings true when applied to the field of education. It goes without saying that the chances for high student achievement increase exponentially with the quality of the school employees. Weak teachers and weak administrators tend to produce weak schools and weak student achievement. This strategy is presented first in order to highlight the importance of school districts recruiting and employing the best available, most highly qualified people to work with children.

Teachers spend the bulk of their time during the work day working with students. Teachers, therefore, make up the bedrock of the instructional activities for students. It seems to follow that the first strategy of a school district should be to focus on teacher quality in order to drive student achievement.

As a principal and as a superintendent, I worked in many school districts across the U.S. and in Japan. The various professional work experiences drove home the fact that many people play roles in the educational process; however, the teacher-quality factor towers high in the process. I am often reminded of the importance of teacher quality based on the outstanding work of one of America's finest teachers, Ted Lega. Ted was the renowned band teacher for twenty-five years at Joliet Central High School while I served as high school principal. As principal, I managed by walking around to keep current on things going on in the various classrooms. Observing the classroom of Ted Lega was always an enriching experience. As a teacher, he used pedagogical methodologies that always resulted in high student performances. Under his leadership, the Joliet High School Symphonic Band was rated exemplary at every festival, contest and concert. For his masterful work as a teacher, Ted was selected as one of the few high school teachers ever inducted into the American Bandmaster Association. As a teacher, he exhibited a quiet manner while utilizing teaching processes that demanded excellence. He did not yell, shout, scream, or demean his students. He simply shared with them his expectations for excellence and he worked with them to reach the level of expectations.

As superintendent in a large urban school district, I had the opportunity to observe hundreds of outstanding teachers motivating students to achieve at very high levels. Many teachers that I observed on a regular basis worked with students before and after regular school hours to ensure that all of their students achieved at high levels. Many teachers expressed to students their expectations and would not be satisfied until every child in the classroom reached the targeted expectations. I recall one teacher expressing his joy in having to teach an Algebra I class for ninth grade students who were mathematically challenged. Using a variety of hands-on manipulatives, balance beam activities, proportionate exercises, and weekend algebra camps, the teacher was able to motivate all of his students to earn high grades in the class by the end of the semester.

Other experiences have shown just the opposite. I have observed teachers who turned off students in mathematics and science classes because of, in some cases, their lack of knowledge of the subject and their inability to communicate with students. All of these highlights of my experiences are being shared to point out the fact that a key strategy for improving student achievement is the employment of excellent teachers. A master teacher is worth more than gold. Students do not hire their teachers. Adults are responsible for the hiring of teachers. Students thus become the captive audience engaged in the learning activities organized by the teachers hired by adults.

Teaching is moving closer now to becoming a true profession instead of a quasi-profession. In an interesting report printed in the 1993 ASCD Yearbook, Linda Darling-Hammond and A. Lin Goodwin present the evolution of the teaching occupation by highlighting the following: "One hundred years ago, teachers needed no more than a grammar school education to teach; fifty years ago, a college education was desirable but not mandatory. Today, most teachers have at least a master's degree.... Since the 1940s, virtually all states have 'raised' standards for entry by regulating teacher education offerings and, more recently, requiring licensing tests."[1] (See Appendix 1 for purported language in the contracts of early teachers.)

Times and conditions have improved somewhat since the early days in the teaching field. Teachers are better organized now with labor unions or associations in most states. Licensing and testing requirements in most states have been ratcheted up in order to weed out possibly incompetent teachers. Colleges of education are working to do a better job of preparing future teachers in the areas of subject content and pedagogy. Most colleges are also becoming sensitive to the important need for training future teachers in the areas of diversity, technology, and interpersonal communication.

In many areas of the country, especially in the large urban cities, teachers are being assigned classes that consist of students from multiple ethnic groups — African Americans, Latin Americans, Asian Americans, and many others generally referred to as minorities. Teachers today must have training in the fundamentals of teaching and sensitivity to all students, especially minority students. Because of the big push in the country to close the gap between the academic performance of white students and minority students, it is becoming important for teachers to have the following preparation as outlined by Howard Hill in his book *Effective Strategies for Teaching Minority Students:*

- Be prepared to teach educationally under-prepared students
- Develop a second language (Spanish, regional dialects)
- Develop street smarts
- Be aware of cultural and ethnic history
- Ethnic literature must be used in teaching whenever possible
- Intercultural differences or idiosyncrasies must be examined and understood
- Find a mentor[2]

Even with the progress that has been made, there still is the issue of the shortage of teachers to serve the schools in the United States. Each year, school districts and states are still issuing emergency teaching permits to uncertified teachers. Paradoxically, the push is to have highly qualified teachers in all classrooms when there is a critical shortage of teachers, especially in such areas as mathematics, science, bilingual education, special education, music, and technology. In many school districts, unfortunately, administrators are happy to get a warm body to cover classes due to the shortage of both certified and substitute teachers. As strange as it may seem, that is the reality of many school situations existing today. I can recall, as superintendent in a school district in California, sending my district recruiting team to the Philippines and England in search of teachers who might become certified in the State of California due to the major shortage of teachers in the state.

It is estimated that there are between 2.2 and 2.6 million teachers now working in schools in the United States.[3] It is further projected that, unless major steps are taken, the supply shortage of teachers could become more acute because colleges are graduating no more than two-thirds of the number of teachers needed. This information is being shared in order to communicate the complexities involved in implementing the strategy of recruiting and employing highly qualified teachers, especially in light of the No Child Left Behind Act.

In many cases, this strategy is easier said than done because of situations beyond the control of the school or school district. The concept still remains as a pivotal strategy for improving student achievement — highly qualified teachers foster improved student achievement.

Highly Qualified Administrators

Highly qualified and strong school administrators are key people in the strategy of improving student achievement. School administrators tend to set the tone for the organizations that they lead. School districts tend to reflect the quality of the leadership of the superintendent/board of education. The local school buildings tend to reflect the leadership of the principal and the building leadership team. The classrooms in the individual school buildings tend to reflect the teachers in the classrooms. Having participated in numerous accreditation team visits and hundreds of school visits as a school superintendent, it is crystal clear to me that quality leadership and organized school administration are very important contributors to improving student achievement.

The old saying, "Where there is no vision, the people perish," is truly apropos to school leadership and administration. The No Child Left Behind Act has ushered in rigorous accountabilities and standards, the likes of which most school administrators have never witnessed before. In college work, the climate is to "publish or perish." Similarly, NCLB now calls for schools to produce continuous improvements in student achievement as measured by state tests or go out of existence. This is heavy pressure and cause for major stress for administrators in the current environment. Local communities are being educated today about the quality of their schools as measured by state standards. The local school administrators and boards of education are having to answer to parents and community citizens about the quality of the schools as portrayed, rightly or wrongly, by local media and NCLB requirements.

With the stakes in public education so high, it is now beneficial for local school districts to focus intensive efforts on recruiting and employing highly qualified administrators. It seems to follow that having highly qualified administrators will greatly enhance the chances for success in businesses and schools. Nationally renowned consultant on educational leadership, Phillip Schlechty, in his book *Schools for the Twenty-first Century: Leadership Imperatives for Education Reform*, states that his "book proceeds from the assumption that the key to school reform is effective leadership."[4]

In the business world, it is common for corporations to seek out, recruit and employ leaders that will bring about improvements in profits for the shareholders. Fortune 500 magazines are replete with hundreds of interesting stories about the efforts of Fortune 500 companies striving to employ highly qualified leaders and administrators. In order to entice successful leaders to join their organizations, most corporations strive to offer excellent salary packages, professional working conditions, and authority to make changes that will result in greater profits and company improvements.

It has been interesting to many people, as they observed over the years the changes of leadership at the giant Coca-Cola soft drink company. Many publications have focused attention on the perceived impact of the various leaders on the Coca-Cola Company. Despite the myriad of elements that did occur, the impressions and focus of many have been based on the bottom-line profits of the company. The CEO of the company took the credit when the profits came in at high levels. The CEO had to also take the heat when profits came in at low levels. Thus, the administrators at Coca-Cola and others in the business world have been forced to be dynamic, creative, strong, innovative and highly qualified in order to meet the challenges inherent in the volatile world of business. And that's the way it is in business today.

The business model of administration is now invading the field of education. Fueled by the injection of new standards, greater competition, higher public expectations for accountability, and the bottom-line business mentality brought on by NCLB, school districts, like big corporations, are now searching for highly qualified administrators. It is becoming clear to many local boards of education that highly qualified school leaders can foster higher student achievement when given proper support, authority, funding and professional respect. Highly qualified administrators usually come with a price. The price often includes the same amenities as expected in the corporate/business world — competitive salary, professional working conditions, and authority to implement changes for improvements in student achievement and the operation of the district. Highly qualified school administrators have usually spent many years in training and in gaining experience related to leadership. Thus, as specialists in the field of education, just like specialists in the medical field and other specialized areas, they are now expecting to be treated with respect. They are now expecting to receive compensation commensurate with their training and position.

Fortunately, most school districts are now realizing that highly qualified teachers and highly qualified administrators are critical parts of the equation for improving student achievement. It is highly unlikely that high student achievement will come about with unqualified teachers and unqualified administrators. Unfortunately, many schools in the country today are employing teachers and administrators who are not highly qualified. In many cases, adults are employing people who are not highly qualified, yet blaming their students for poor academic results.

It has been interesting observing the school administrative culture in the United States over the past decades. It has been interesting observing the paradoxes, improvements, expectations and focus areas in the field of school administration. Historically, early leaders in the various communities were the school administrators. With the growth of the common school concept, groups of farmers or business people usually came together and pooled their dollars to build local schoolhouses and to employ one or more people to teach in the schools. The local leaders usually met to pay the bills, fix the schoolhouses and to plan. As states began passing legislation and codes for schools, local leaders began electing boards of education and hiring specific people charged to fulfill the growing administrative functions of school districts and local schools. The city of Buffalo, New York, is recognized as the first city to have hired a superintendent to function as the administrator of a school district in the 1800s. This bit of historical information was important since I served as a superintendent of schools in Buffalo. In the early days, as schools grew larger with students, staffing and building sizes increasing, the need developed for the employment of building principals to administer the local schools.

The early days of education in the United States were characterized by many paradoxical situations. The nation in the early days was agrarian in focus. People worked the land by farming to eke out their existence. Buffalo and wild game were plentiful. The focus in many areas was on settling and clearing wooded areas for the expansion of farming. For centuries, slavery was constitutionally justified, especially in the South. Thus, many people of color and others from very low socio-economic strata were not allowed the opportunities to access academic and leadership training. Segregation was expected and accepted in the majority of the states. A country that professed freedom in its early days was concurrently enforcing slavery and barring millions of people from educational opportunities, especially during the agrarian period and early industrial period.

Historically, the Industrial Revolution period in the United States fostered the opportunities for more people to access education, both children and adults. The Morrill Act of 1862 established land grant colleges in every state to provide training in agricultural arts, vocational training, teacher training, mechanical arts, military arts and other areas.[5] Normal colleges were established for the training of teachers and African Americans. Two tiers of colleges existed, one for whites and one for African Americans, then called "Negroes" and "Coloreds." Some of the normal colleges were also organized to train students in agriculture, vocations, and teaching. The normal colleges and land grant colleges became the sources for the majority of teachers and school administrators in the country for a century. It should be noted that during the years of segregated schools, white people served as principals of white schools and African Americans and other people of color served as principals of their schools, especially in the southern states. In the northern states, people of color had very few opportunities to serve as school administrators until the initiation of the civil rights movement in the late 1960s.

For more than a century, the general progression for school administrators followed the path of service as teacher, assistant principal, principal, superintendent. In many states during the early days of the country, especially in the southern states, school superintendents were elected countywide with one superintendent serving as the administrator over all of the schools and principals in the county. In many cases in the early days, the position of superintendent was a political position. Today, nearly all superintendents are selected and employed by boards of education and, in few cases, by city mayors.

The road to respect for highly qualified school administrators has been long and filled with interesting elements. Early school administrators were paid poorly and often had very poor working conditions. In many areas, school administrators were asked to lead schools and school districts with inadequate funding, inadequate school facilities, and many unqualified teachers. In some areas of the country in the early days, a person could become a teacher or an administrator with only one or two years of college since college degrees were not required for employment in schools. In early African American schools, teachers were employed if they had two years of high school, a high school diploma, or standing in the community as a preacher —

it was assumed that preachers had to be able at least to read the Bible. During the Industrial Revolution period, most school administrators, especially in the minority communities, were preachers or members of families highly respected and politically connected. The title of "Reverend" in early days commanded great respect and opened the doors for minority teachers possessing the religious title to be assigned as administrators to schools in minority communities.

The transition from the Industrial Revolution to the technological and information period witnessed many changes in the areas of teaching and school administration. From 1956 to the present, the licensing and certification of teachers and school administrators became ever-increasing for a variety of reasons. With the launching by Russia of the Sputnik space orbiter, the American education community and government began focusing greater attention on improving education for a greater mass of students, especially in the areas of mathematics and science. A host of innovations invaded the school curricula from New Math to required science instruction for students. The Federal government provided National Defense Student Loans and a host of new programs designed to jump start higher quality education and expansion of educational opportunities for more students at all levels. Community colleges were organized. This writer had the fortunate experience of serving as high school principal for four years at Joliet Township Central High Schools, the site of the first community college in the country. The civil rights movement leaders marched and demanded the integration of public schools and colleges, high quality education at all levels, and proper service at lunch counters, restaurants, hotels, and work sites.

With increased training for teachers and school administrators, seeds began to be planted for greater accountability from schools. School groups began organizing labor unions for teachers and administrators to develop rights and protection through contracts, as the seeds of accountability and the professional nature of education began germinating. The recognition of school administration had arrived as major universities formally implemented degrees in school administration to prepare mostly proactive teachers to become school administrators and superintendents.

The gradual progression of the business model into the field of education, as exhibited in the protocols of the No Child Left Behind Act of 2001, has had a chilling impact on the area of school administration. The old liberal arts model of teaching for teaching's sake has been replaced with teaching and leadership to meet state and local learning standards and benchmarks. States, boards of education and local communities are now issued a plethora of data about student performance, heretofore mostly seen by selected people in school organizations. School administrators are being held accountable, along with teachers, for developing and delivering curricula that result in progressive increases in student achievement as measured by predetermined state tests.

To reach the ever-increasing benchmarks in student achievement, school boards are not only now seeking to recruit and hire highly qualified teachers, they are intensely seeking and hiring highly qualified school administrators and superintendents. The stakes are high for local school districts and individual schools. The stakes are even higher for school administrators. The landmark impact of NCLB is massive. School administrators can no longer use averages and aggregate test scores to show how great their schools are. With NCLB, student performance must be exhibited in multiple ways — according to race, disabilities, bilingual status, socio-economic status, and other factors. Failure to make adequate yearly progress as prescribed by the plan organized by individual states could have definite consequences. The carrot-and-stick principle has entered the field of education. Federal dollars continue to be awarded as entitlement funds to qualified schools. The future calls for those schools receiving federal entitlement/categorical funds to produce higher student test scores or go out of business. This sounds familiar to many business minded people — make a profit or go out of business.

"But wait one cotton-picking minute!" some school administrators forcefully exclaim. "Why would anyone want to be a school administrator in this day and time when a law, NCLB, mandates but fails to properly fund the mandates?" Fair question?

Other pertinent questions that abound in the circle of existing and potential administrators include the following:

- Why would I want to work as an administrator without the authority to make decisions for the school or district that I am hired to lead?
- Why would I want to work in an environment where some board of education members micromanage my building operations?
- Why would I want to work in a school where there are inadequate funds for instructional supplies, books, computers, and building repairs?
- Why would I want to work in an environment of heavy district politics rather than major focus on the things best for students?
- Why would I want to work in an environment without highly qualified staff to help reach the objectives for students?

These and a host of other questions are now being posed by many people who view the field of education administration as a quagmire filled with disrespect, stress, unrealistic expectations, low pay, inadequate funding, and generally unprofessional working conditions. Thus, most highly academically qualified people choose other professional fields. Some ask the question, "Can you really blame them?"

Writer Warren Bennis penned some interesting thoughts about leadership in his book entitled *Why Leaders Can't Lead.* One of his more insightful thoughts was presented in the following pronouncement: "An unconscious conspiracy in contemporary society prevents leaders — no matter what their original vision — from taking charge and making changes. Within any organization, an entrenched bureaucracy with a commitment to the status quo undermines the unwary leader."[6] Having served on the faculties of M.I.T., Harvard, Boston University, as provost at the University of Buffalo, and president of the University of Cincinnati, Bennis aptly described the complexities involved school and business leadership based on his experiences in the workplace. Having served as a high school principal and superintendent in four school districts, I concur with his notion that administration and leadership of contemporary organizations can be characterized as turbulent, sacrificial, and deteriorating in nature. His chapter on "When There Are Too Many Chiefs" provides interesting insights into the realistic culture of leadership and administration that often discourage many people from seeking administrative positions.[7]

The answer to the issue of highly qualified teachers, administrators and other staff for education is controversial and highly personal. On one hand, we all want the best education possible for all students. On the other hand, many people recognize that the field of education has many challenges that must be addressed by people on many levels from governments, boards of education, local taxpaying citizens, parents, community leaders, civic groups, religious organizations, colleges, and many other groups. The interesting fact is that the issue of improving student achievement is predominantly in the jurisdiction of adults, not students. Can students truly be held responsible if adults in communities hire teachers and administrators that are not highly qualified? Can students be held responsible if adults in their community provide them with inadequate school supplies, poor-quality instructional equipment and poor-quality school buildings? Can students be held responsible for adults not providing proper home care? Can students be held responsible for adults sending them to school without proper clothes, meals, and other support?

The Search Institute has conducted extensive research on many of the topics posed by teachers and administrators. Based on its findings, the institute has been advocating that adults take responsibility for providing children with forty "Developmental Assets" during the elementary school age years. The institute has been advocating strongly that teachers and administrators will be more effective in doing their jobs in schools when adults in the community provide the proper developmental assets.[8] It should not take rocket science intelligence to figure out the answers to many of the questions posed in this section. It seems quite clear that the first and foremost essential strategy for improving student achievement at any time is the employment of highly qualified teachers and school administrators. Student achievement is to a great degree proportionate to the quality of the teachers and administrators working in the schools. It seems to follow that students with highly qualified teachers and administrators tend to achieve at high levels. Conversely, students in schools with poor quality teachers and administrators have less chance for excelling at high levels. One of the preeminent education scholars, John Goodlad, echoes the ideas of this chapter by suggesting that "there is a natural connection between good teachers and good schools."[9] Goodlad warns, however, that everyone should remember the following: 1) "it is reasonable to assume a long-term relationship between a good school system and a vibrant economy;" and 2) "schools are only part of the education system....They can only supplement homes, religious institutions, and all the rest."[10]

It should be noted that the challenge of having and improving the academic performance of all students is not simple. It is complex, intricate, dynamic and ever-changing. There are many pieces in the puzzle of strategies for improving student achievements. Let us now move to strategy number two.

Footnotes

[1]Linda Darling-Hammond and Lin Goodwin, "Progress Toward Professionalism in Teaching," *The 1993 Association for Supervision and Curriculum Development Yearbook* (Arlington: Association for Supervision and Curriculum Development, 1993), 26.

[2]Howard Hill, *Effective Strategies for Teaching Minority Students* (Bloomington: National Educational Service, 1989), 2-3.

[3]Linda Darling-Hammond and Lin Goodwin, "Progress Toward Professionalism in Teaching," 29.

[4]Phillip Schlechty, *Schools for the Twenty-first Century* (San Francisco: Jossey-Bass Publishers, 1990), 8.

[5]Robert Church, *Education in the United States* (New York: The Free Press, 1976), 9-13.

[6]Warren Bennis, *Why Leaders Can't Lead* (San Francisco: Jossey-Bass Publishers, 1989), xii.

[7]Ibid., 76-80.

[8] Search Institute, *Forty Developmental Assets for Elementary-Age Children Report* (Minneapolis: The Search Institute), 1-8.

[9]John Goodlad, *Teachers for our Nation's Schools* (San Francisco: Jossey-Bass Publisher, 1990), xi.

[10]Ibid., 17.

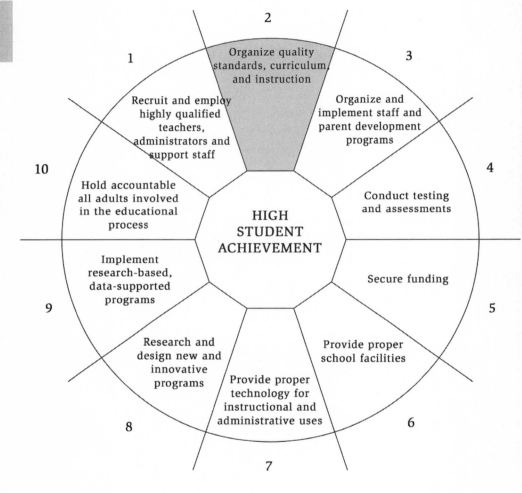

Ten essential strategies for adults
supporting high student achievement.

STRATEGY NUMBER TWO:

Organize High Quality Standards, Curriculum and Instruction

Most of us tend to be able to determine when things and situations are of high quality. Most people tend to be able to tell over time whether things and situations have grounding in solid or weak standards. When we shop or go out to restaurants, we can tell from many factors the stores and restaurants that have high or low standards. When shopping or going out to eat, we consider such things as (1) quality of service; (2) quality of merchandise or food; (3) appearance of employees, facilities, merchandise, food, cleanliness; (4) climate and environment of the establishment. As human beings, we have the intuitive instinct to determine for ourselves the quality of things around us every day. We can usually determine when things are presented based on certain standards. For example, when we walk into such stores and restaurants as Neiman Marcus, Bose, Wal-Mart, Kroger, Lowery's, McDonald's, White Castle, Sears or J.C. Penney, we can instantly observe their offerings, presentations and services. In other words, we can tell to a great degree that their operations are based on certain standards. They are held to and expected to meet certain levels of quality.

On another level, many of us have been intrigued with the standards in the area of higher education. Of course, certain

2

standards in higher education have been influenced and adjusted based on new insights, politics and new leadership. For many people, the pinnacle of higher education in the United States is in the universities — Michigan, Harvard, Yale, Howard, Virginia State, New York University, USC, UCLA, the University of Chicago and a host of other outstanding universities, many of which I have been associated with either as a student, researcher, or supporter. All of the great universities have high standards. Just like businesses, the universities' quality can be described based on their adherence to certain standards. Mention Harvard Business School or Kennedy School of Government at Harvard, and informed people will attest to their quality and tradition of excellence. Mention the University of Michigan, and informed people will attest to high quality in research, professors, training of educational/school leaders, science, athletics, music, business, technology and a host of other areas. I often speak highly of the standards at such schools as Michigan, Virginia State University, and Harvard, having earned degrees or certificates from them. As a writer, researcher, and educator, I can express from personal experiences that the standards and training provided at those institutions are *par excellence.*

Relating all of the above to strategies for improving student achievement seems most logical. In education today, schools are being mandated to educate all students to standards usually developed at the state level. Since education is delegated as a state function by the Constitution of the United States of America, individual states have taken the mantle and established state standards for learning to be instituted in local schools. States have established various methods of monitoring and assessing the levels of commitment to their standards by local schools. In the circle of educational professionals, views

Organize High Quality Standards, Curriculum and Instruction

vary relative to the quality of the standards for education that have been developed by the various states. Further, views vary relative to the impact of the standards on local districts and schools. Of course, the current concept of No Child Left Behind is quite simple: all school districts and schools are to develop curriculum based on the prescribed state standards. Just like the process of implementing the standards used by institutions of higher learning, retail businesses and restaurants, local school districts are now being expected to operate by following and implementing prescribed standards, especially related to student achievement, teacher quality and curriculum. Writers Marc Tucker and Judy Codding have contexturized standards in education as meaning "an obsession with results, with reaching predetermined levels of student achievement. This requires an unrelenting determination to get virtually all students to high achievement levels, whatever that takes."[1]

Historically, one could trace the roots of the standards efforts in education back to many high profile actions in the United States. Most of the actions were sparked by the civil rights movement in this country. First, one could relate the decision of the 1954 *Brown v. Board of Education* case as a benchmark. In that case, it was determined by the United States Supreme Court that separate but equal schools based on race were not constitutional.[2] That decision ignited the long civil rights movement that was led by the National Association for the Advancement of Colored People (NAACP), Southern Christian Leadership Conference (SCLC), and other organizations with the mission of fostering equal rights and the integration of public schools in the United States, particularly in the areas south of the Mason-Dixon Line (the boundary line between Pennsylvania and Maryland that divided free and slave states). The underlying concept was that the standards for edu-

2

cation at the time, 1954, for white students were different and higher than the standards for Negro/colored students. Some poignant examples of standards that existed related to such basic things as books, equipment, and teacher and administrative compensation. With books, the standard and practice in most Southern public schools prior to 1954 called for new books to be first used by students in schools with the white students. After the books were used by the white students for two to three years, they were then to be sent to the schools for use by Negro/colored school students. Believe it or not, that was the standard and practice. Thus, Negro/colored students often had to learn from books replete with wear, marks, and sometimes torn and missing pages. Thus, the loud cry rose from civil rights groups that separate was not equal in most schools in the Southern states. In the area of compensation, in most Southern states, Negro/colored teachers and administrators were paid a much lower rate than their counterparts in white schools. Pay rates were held secret and not made public. Negro/colored teachers and administrators feared requesting such information about pay comparison with whites because they could lose their jobs. In the Southern states before 1954, the standard and practice called for white students to always have the best and Negro/colored students to have only the basics. Fortunately, the Black colleges of the period stepped forward and provided the support and higher education for a host of students of color. This writer had the good fortune of having parents, both of whom were educators, who experienced and witnessed all of the unequal treatment of students and educators of color.

Writers Gary Orfield and Susan Eaton followed the integration efforts after the Brown decision. They reported that "contrary to a popular misrepresentation, in many school districts throughout the nation school desegregation was successfully achieved."[3]

As superintendent of the Buffalo Public Schools, I had the honor of having Gary Orfield serve as a consultant and resource as the district worked to comply with a federal court desegregation order. For many years, I witnessed firsthand the complexities involved in fostering school integration in a school district mired in *de facto* and *de jure* segregation.

Another benchmark in standards development in the education movement was the publication of the *A Nation at Risk Report* of 1983. Basically, the report indicated that students in American schools were not performing at acceptable levels and reforms and standards were needed in American schools to improve student performance.[4] The report presented disturbing inadequacies in the educational process related to curriculum content, achievement expectations, time in school, quality of teachers and teaching.

The governors from most states jumped on the bandwagon as education governors. Many mayors became education mayors and began seeking control of the school districts within their cities — Chicago, New York, Cleveland, Boston, Detroit, Buffalo, Rochester, and many others. Some of the mayors were successful in brokering state legislation granting them total or major control of public schools within their municipalities. For example, the Illinois state legislative body granted Mayor Daley virtually full control of the then-perceived as failing Chicago Public Schools, dubbed by some as the worst school system in the nation.[5] As a high school principal in Joliet, Illinois, as an assistant superintendent in West Aurora, Illinois, and as a superintendent of schools at North Chicago, Illinois, this writer witnessed firsthand the first major infusion of the standards movement into education. In Chicago, the mayor appointed and

2

routinely fired school superintendents and their staffs. Many executive administrators in Chicago worked at the pleasure of the mayor just like city executive staff members.

Like the mayor of Chicago, the mayor of Cleveland was granted power over the Cleveland Public Schools. Thus, the superintendent of the Cleveland Public Schools was appointed by the mayor and worked at his pleasure. The mayor of New York City was granted increased power over the New York City schools and he appointed the superintendent/chancellor to lead the school district. As the superintendent of the Buffalo, New York, school district, this writer witnessed firsthand the efforts of the mayors of Buffalo, Rochester, Syracuse, and New York City to take control of the districts. Only the mayor of New York City was successful in gaining control of the schools. All of the other mayors were blocked in gaining control of their city schools, due largely to the political work done by the Honorable Arthur Eve, long-term deputy speaker of the New State Assembly.

The National Conference of Governors held a series of meetings during the 1980s and 1990s. The outcome of the meetings of the governors was a commitment to develop educational standards for schools in their individual states. The governors were influenced greatly to develop education standards by many top business leaders and CEOs of the period. Many business leaders began writing books and making speeches about the need to improve standards to improve education and schools in the country. Most notable as a banner carrier for higher student achievement from the business sector was Louis V. Gerstner, Jr., Chairman and CEO of IBM. For many years, Mr. Gerstner proclaimed in speeches and books his concepts for reforming schools to improve student achievement. His book, *Reinventing Education: Entrepreneurship in America's Public*

Organize High Quality Standards, Curriculum and Instruction

Schools, received national attention from business leaders, educators and governmental leaders.[6]

The election of George W. Bush as President of the United States marked the movement from the "carrot era" (1980-2000) in standards to the "carrot-and-stick" era (starting 2001). The No Child Left Behind Act of 2001 is hailed by many as one of the pivotal federal laws related to education for the United States. The law mandated a sweeping series of requirements for states to implement in order to receive Title I federal funds. Embedded in the law was the requirement for states to develop and implement educational standards for the schools to implement. Failure to implement the requirements of the law by a particular state would result in the denial of federal Title I funds to that state. Because most states depended on the Title I funds to assist in educating students, nearly all states moved with haste to develop educational standards and to meet the other requirements of the law in order to be in compliance with the law.

To some states, statewide standards for education were new. To other states, the NCLB requirements for standards were deemed in line with good educational practices that had been ongoing for decades. A key factor of NCLB was the nationwide expectation for all states to develop and implement educational standards. To receive federal Title I funds, school districts would have to implement the state standards.

The governors of most states assigned the task of developing educational standards to their state departments of education. The education departments of the states convened various task groups to write the standards. Most states wrote standards first for the core areas of language arts/reading/writing and mathematics. It was most logical for the states to complete the standards in language arts and mathematics because the Title I goals were to foster improvements in those two academic areas, espe-

2

2

cially for students who qualified for remedial intervention and support. The development of standards in most states followed the progression of language arts and mathematics first, then sciences, social studies, the arts, physical education, career education, technology and other areas.

Today, school districts interested in improving student achievement as measured by their state are investing great amount of time and resources in understanding clearly the standards for education from the state departments of education. Using the state standards as the major starting point, school districts are moving to the important phase of writing curriculum aligned to state standards. In an era of high stakes testing, school leaders now realize that curriculum must be aligned and taught to state standards. Gone are the days when school boards allowed all teachers to teach whatever they felt inclined to teach. The NCLB Act has now ushered in state standards and, in some cases, state grade level curriculum. The local school districts must meet and comply with mandates in multiple areas. Thus, a key strategy for improving student achievement in the present period is to know the standards and to ensure that the curriculum is standards-driven.

Curriculum

School districts and schools exist primarily to deliver a high quality curriculum to students. The curriculum is developed by adults for students. The students make up the captive audience mandated to participate and learn the curriculum organized by adults. Students thus are at the mercy, to a great degree, of the adults who develop, fund and implement the curriculum for them. In districts where adults pay poor attention to curriculum, in most cases student achievement tends to be low.

Organize High Quality Standards, Curriculum and Instruction

Conversely, in districts where major attention is paid to curriculum, student achievement tends to be high. The central theme in the strategy for improving student achievement is high quality adult involvement in developing and implementing curriculum. This strategy can be accelerated with insightful understanding of the nature of curriculum. What is curriculum? How can the curriculum be delivered to students to foster high achievement? Let us explore some current understandings of curriculum.

Curriculum is the totality of all that is organized, written and unwritten, academic and non-academic, for students to learn while associated with a school or a school district. The curriculum, in a business sense, is the product that schools offer to students and parents. Thus, the heart and soul of a school district can be determined to a large degree by the curriculum developed by the adults associated with the school. Fenwick English writes that "the function of curriculum is to shape the work of teachers by focusing and connecting it as a kind of work plan in schools."[7]

For centuries, curriculum has been the topic for research and discussion. Many great minds have taken time to delve into this crucial area of education. Historical information shows that as early as the Greek civilization, the curriculum for students of the time was deemed important. During that period, it was determined that students had to study academics, the arts, and physical development in order to be well rounded and properly educated. The curriculum of that period focused on developing the mind, body, and talent. The educational process of that time was rigorous, with intensive drills, memorization and teaching of concepts for application of knowledge. Many great theses were written about the core curriculum that students should have in order to function properly in the society of that time.

2

Students who were selected for formal education were expected not only to master the academic and artistic aspects of the curriculum, they were also expected to develop their physique highly in order to serve in later years in the athletic and military competitions of the time. The Greeks are credited with having started the Olympic competitions that continue even into the twenty-first century.

From the Greeks to today, the following four critical questions about curriculum are still being pondered:

- What should be taught?
- When and in what order?
- How should the curricular elements be taught?
- How will the curriculum be evaluated and students assessed?

As to "what should be taught" in the curriculum of schools in the United States, one can find a historical pattern of many pathways that eventually led to the present configurations of skills outlined for students to learn. The early settlers generally taught students in small groups when time permitted. They focused on a curriculum of basic reading, writing and arithmetic.[8] Parents of that era taught students about farming, business, trade, religion, social skills related to the affective domain, and behavior. Many students of that era were taught language arts-related skills in order to read the Bible.[9] The Bible was one of the most read books of that generation because it provided hope and religious concepts to the people who were struggling to establish living conditions. The history books of education are replete with the early establishment of schools by volunteers, church groups, civic groups and eventually by states.[10]

Even with the gradual organization of schools, the question for discussion still remained: what should be taught? Many answers to that question existed during the early days of schools in the United States. In general, most schools focused on reading, writing and arithmetic, the "three Rs." During the early days of the country, many students worked most of the time in the fields or family businesses. There was not abundant time for schooling. Thus, when students did attend school, their time was focused on a core curriculum of the three Rs. Time did not permit most students to have an expanded curriculum like the Greeks.

It should be noted that the curriculum-content issue became prominent in the late 1800s and early 1900s. As the United States was being transformed from heavily agrarian to an emerging industrial nation, schools were following that change, especially in the area of curriculum. In organization, the curriculum that evolved mirrored the assembly-line approach that called for students to attend school for twelve years and to study an expanded series of courses. Added to the curriculum were such specific subjects as science, vocational education, home economics, arts, music, physical education, and social studies. A review of the history of curriculum in the United States shows that the curriculum offerings in U.S. schools expanded rapidly over the period beginning in the 1900s. Fostering the curriculum expansion were such inventions as electricity, automobiles, improved printing presses, radio, airplanes, telephones, refrigeration, establishment of many colleges, and a host of other developments. The curriculum had to change based on the demands of the times during the early 1900s.

One of the educational theorists who had a major impact on schools of the 1900s was John Dewey. Labeled later as an educational progressivist, Dewey wrote and taught extensively the progressive philosophy related to teaching and curriculum. He had the good fortune of doing research and teaching at two

2

great universities, the University of Chicago and the University of Michigan. The curriculum concepts from his work at the two universities propelled him into the national spotlight in the field of educational philosophy. Accepted by many and rejected by some, his curriculum concept called for schools to provide students a curriculum based heavily on the interests and experiences of the students. He suggested that the curriculum should have certain conceptual content that would spark the investigative and research curiosity of students. He recommended that the role of the teacher be transformed from the deliverer of knowledge to that of instructional coach in the curriculum process. His proposed curriculum would encompass the core academic areas, the arts, and vocational education all fused into a model of research and investigation based on research and the interests of students. The Dewey-based progressive curriculum was a vast break from the traditional curriculum because it called for a change from the rigidity of the old curriculum to one with great flexibility and less rigidity. It should be noted that the influence of Dewey on curriculum was instrumental in allowing and justifying in the minds of many the inclusion of a vast number of new areas of study and courses based on the theory that the curriculum should mirror the interests and experience of students. Thus, one can trace a litany of new courses in the curriculum of many schools that could be rationalized as having been influenced by the philosophy of John Dewey.[11]

It should be noted that the technical and governance aspects of curriculum also have a history. As states assumed their responsibilities in education as provided by the U. S. Constitution, legislation was passed in nearly all states empowering local boards of education to organize and adapt curriculum and to govern local schools districts. The theory underpinning the early curriculum design called for local control of schools.[12] The concept took root in communities across the country and remained as a source of discussion even until the present time. From the late 1800s to the mid 1950s, local school boards operated with extensive control over curriculum, taxes, personnel, and length of the school year, with very minimal state and federal intrusion.[13]

It has been interesting to note that heavy state and federal intrusion into local school curriculum can be traced to results of *Brown v. Board of Education* in 1954 and the Russian launch of Sputnik. Those two events commenced a series of actions. The Brown case forced school districts to end the practice of segregation based on race in the organization of schools. It also forced school districts to provide real equity in the curricular offerings in all schools. Prior to the directives from the court in the Brown case, schools in many states, especially in Southern states, were organized based on race. Negro/colored students were required to attend schools organized solely for that race. It was illegal in most states, especially in the Southern states, for African American students to attend schools with white students. It was the practice of the times, before the Brown directive, for white schools in most areas in the country to have more advanced curriculum with accompanying supplies, books, equipment and teachers. In most of the schools that were attended by African American students, the content of the curriculum content was often only basic in nature and, in many cases, these schools lacked proper supplies, books, and equipment. Further, teachers were often forced to teach subjects for which they were not properly trained. That was the acceptable practice of that era. The Brown decision provided the federal and state governments the legal backing that was needed to begin the long process of ending racial discrimination in schools. Many people recall the ugly mob actions that occurred

2

in many areas of the South when the federal government was called into action to enforce the court orders and mandates for the integration of the schools.

Fortunately for the country, the Brown case began the process of providing all students with opportunities to learn curriculum with less chance of inequity. Thurgood Marshall and all of the early pioneers for equal access to quality educational curriculum can be credited today for their valiant actions. It should be noted that Thurgood Marshall went on after the Brown case to become the first African American to serve on the United States Supreme Court.[14]

When the Russians beat the United States in becoming the first nation to launch a spacecraft into space, the federal government began major actions to revise the curriculum of K-12 schools and higher education. The launching of the Sputnik spacecraft by the Russians set off a series of unprecedented actions related to curriculum in the United States. Because of the perception that the Russians had become more advanced in the sciences with their educational system, the federal government in the U.S. began forcing schools and colleges to revise curriculum to focus greater time and training in the areas of mathematics, science, and the new field of technology. In the late 1950s and through the 1960s, most schools districts changed their curriculum to include new mathematics and new sciences. Computers and handheld calculators became part of the education culture. In many states, students were required to complete increased instructional time in a battery of science classes. The federal government increased significantly the amount of grants for science and technology curriculum research. After Sputnik, the country was shrouded in an aura of concern about the defense of the United States. Some people believed that the United States had to move quickly to improve the curriculum of schools in the areas of science, mathematics and technology in order to develop the skills necessary to defend the county. Thus, the federal government began providing a large amount of dollars to colleges for grants, student loans and projects under the auspices of the National Defense Student Loan and Grants program. The funds were allocated in a liberal manner to encourage colleges to have proper resources to encourage students of all economic levels and races to enter college. Generous funds and programs were available to students who were interested in college scholarships, especially to students interested in studying the areas of the sciences, mathematics and technology.

The Brown case and Sputnik are considered by many as the two historical events that ignited increased involvement by state and federal governments into the curriculum and general operation of schools. Other notable historical events can also be linked with accelerating the involvement of government into school curriculum. The Civil Rights Act legislation signed by President Lyndon Johnson, federal special education regulations, and many other actions had direct or indirect impact on the curriculum of schools. Local control of curriculum began being diminished with the mandates from state and national agencies. It should be noted that the state of Hawaii has always had a state curriculum and has been the longtime example of full state control of schools. Over the latter decades of the 1900s, the influences of the business community, state and federal mandates have evolved into the No Child Left Behind (NCLB) era. Across the country, the curriculum of school districts is being closely aligned to state standards at the impetus of the No Child Left Behind Act of 2001.

Based on the carrot and the stick aspects of NCLB, school districts that are interested in receiving Title I funds must com-

2

ply with the mandates of the federal law and state guidelines. Because most school districts have grown accustomed to the financial resources available through Title I and other federal and state funds, and because most school districts are constantly in need of additional funds, their tendencies are to do everything necessary to comply with the mandates of the funding, governing agencies. NCLB in theory calls for school districts to align their curriculum to state standards. The legislation calls for annual testing of students with the objective of having all students showing documented achievement at state-developed proficiency levels by the year 2014. The objective is lofty and ambitious. The objective is also having a major impact on the curriculum of most school districts. Based on data from the annual state tests that are being administered, school districts are working rapidly to align the following three areas: 1) curriculum, 2) instruction, and 3) assessment/testing. These three areas are being organized based on the standards of the individual states.

NCLB has ushered in full implementation of the educational triad so ably outlined by Fenwick English (see below).[15]

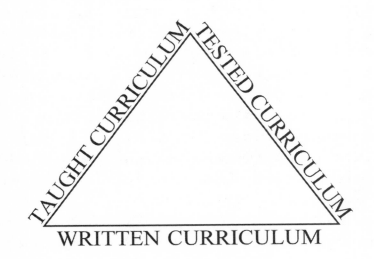

Organize High Quality Standards,
Curriculum and Instruction

The curriculum aspect of the triangle deals with the written curriculum. The local school district still has the major responsibility of organizing and writing the formal curriculum for the district based on state standards, federal guidelines, and laws. Local school curriculum committees in most school districts now have the awesome tasks of learning the state standards and then organizing the various concepts and skill sets to be taught by teachers, learned by students, and assessed based on a state-designed test. The results from the state test must show improvements in test scores annually as gauged by the state plan. Believe me, we are truly now in a period of high-stakes testing in public education. In the state of Michigan, schools that are not meeting the proper levels of student achievement on the state test are called "high priority schools."[16] These schools are given intensive support from the local and state levels. The schools have to organize written improvement plans, receive outside consultation, and implement strict adherence to the curriculum and the instructional pacing plan.

All of the preceding information has been presented in order to show the complex web inherent in the contemporary curriculum. Today, as in past times, the ultimate objective of curriculum is to present an organized series of concepts and skills for students to research, master and apply to life. The reality of life, however, is that today's curriculum has to be fashioned in a manner that ensures students master the skills tested on the state test. Just as importantly, today's curriculum must guarantee that students are prepared for life after high school. Curriculum in contemporary schools requires leadership from one person or a group of people. Curriculum without leadership can be analogous to a ship without a rudder. Thus, curriculum leadership and development are key elements in the educational process for students.[17]

2

Yes, many people today call curriculum "high stakes" for many reasons. First, rightly or wrongly, some people are being fired based on test scores, poor curriculum organization, and poor delivery of curriculum. Yes, many parents now select schools based on the test scores of the schools. Yes, parents now have choices and rights to move their children from schools that are deemed low-performing. Yes, school funding is aligned to student enrollment for a district. Schools must now operate with the sensitivities of business and education or risk losing their customers (students and parents) and funding. The curriculum is an essential element in the complex and fragile web of fostering high student achievement. Following are some of the technical areas associated with contemporary curriculum culture:

Cognitive Curriculum is the listing of the academic skills and concepts that all students are expected to learn while enrolled in the schools in the district. The cognitive domain in education is usually given most attention in the field of education. The cognitive domain of the curriculum is usually written in detail.

Affective Curriculum is the listing of the emotional, attitudinal, behavioral, and inter-personal skills that students are expected to exhibit. The affective domain is often not written in the curriculum as explicitly as is the cognitive domain. However, both are important elements in the overall curriculum.

Curriculum Spiraling is a process of integrating specific concepts and skills at different grade levels during the years of schooling. For example, geometric shapes might be taught to students for a period of time at every grade level leading to the formal enrollment of the students in a geometry class.

Geometry is thus spiraled from grade K to grade 9, or whenever the class is offered to students.

Curriculum Sequencing is similar to spiraling. Sequencing calls for the gradual increase in difficulty of the skill or concept presented annually. The sequencing concept calls for moving from the general to the specific related to a learning skill.

Curriculum Backloading is an overall curriculum planning process focusing on exit skills that students are expected to master in a school district. The process of back-loading calls for the school district to determine what skills are to be taught, at what grade levels the skills will be taught, and for how long the skills will be taught. The back-loading process fosters accountability to the public relative to delivery of the skills for students to master.

Curriculum Pacing is a process of organizing the schedule for the teaching of specific concepts and skills. The instructional pacing schedule is usually written and followed in order to foster coverage of the various learning activities outlined for the year. Pacing charts tend to improve management of instructional time.

Curriculum Articulation is the process of teachers communicating about curriculum at grade level and across grade levels. For example, high school math teachers spend time talking to middle and elementary school teachers about various aspects in the math curriculum for two-way communications.

Curriculum Mapping is integrating spiraling, sequencing, backloading, pacing and articulation combined into one process that results in a master plan for curriculum, a process analogous to mapping out a trip on a road map. Mapping is very time consuming and intense. Mapping, when done properly, is the most effective process to foster accountability, time management, learning, pacing, articulation and improved student achievement. Different forms of curriculum mapping exist, from simple to complex.

The general and technical aspects of curriculum all involve adults. Adults plan the curriculum. Adults write the curriculum. Students tend to suffer when adults fail to properly complete the curriculum work required to foster student learning. When students enroll in schools, they make up a captive audience forced to enjoy, endure, learn, or withdraw from a curriculum organized by adults. To a large degree, the adults involved in the curriculum hold the key to improving student achievement, based on their almost complete control of the curriculum. Thus, adults hold the heart and soul of schools, the curriculum. In schools where adults have taken the necessary time to develop outstanding curriculum, students tend to improve in achievement. Of course, effective curriculum development does not just occur by happenstance; it requires commitment and structured staff development.

Footnotes

[1] Marc Tucker and Judy Codding, *Standards for our Schools: How to Set Them, Measure Them, and Reach Them* (San Francisco: Jossey-Bass, 1998), 21.

[2] Robert Church. *Education in the United States* (New York: The Free Press, 1976), 444-446.

[3] Gary Orfield, Susan Eaton and the Harvard Project on School Desegregation, *Dismantling Desegregation: The Quiet Reversal of Brown v. Board of Education* (New York: The New Press, 1996), viii.

[4] David Berliner and Bruce Biddle, *The Manufactured Crisis: Myths, Fraud, and the Attack on America's Public Schools* (New York: Addison-Wesley Publishing Company, 1995), 3.

[5] Rosetta Vasquez, Reforming Chicago Public Schools: The Intended and Unintended Consequences (DeKalb, IL: LEPS Press, 1994), 63-64.

Organize High Quality Standards, Curriculum and Instruction

[6]Louis V. Gerstner, Jr., Chairman and CEO of IBM, Reinventing Education: Entrepreneurship in America's Public Schools (New York: Penguin Books, 1994), 67-86.

[7]Fenwick English, *Deciding What to Teach and Test: Developing, Aligning, and Auditing the Curriculum* (Thousand Oaks: Corwin Press, 2000), xiv.

[8]Robert Church, Education in the United States, 19.

[9]Ibid., 19.

[10]Ibid., 3-84.

[11]John Dewey.

[12]Robert Church, *Education in the United States*, 10.

[13]Ibid., 10.

[14]Harry Ploski and James Williams, Editors, Reference Library of Black America, Volume II (Gale Research, 1990), 344.

[15]Fenwick English, *Deciding What to Teach and Test*, 64.

[16]Based on the recommendation of James Harris, the governor of Michigan directed that schools that did not make their annual yearly progress goal be identified as "high priority schools," instead of "failing schools."

[17]Leo Bradley, *Curriculum Leadership and Development Handbook* (Englewood Cliffs: Prentice-Hall, 1985), 3.

2

Ten essential strategies for adults
supporting high student achievement.

STRATEGY NUMBER THREE:

Organize and Implement Staff and Parent Development Programs

The two groups that tend to have the greatest impact on the learning of students are parents and school teachers. Parents are the first teachers of children. Parents teach children skills in the affective and cognitive domains from an early age. In the affective area, parents teach children how to behave at home and in public. They teach children such skills as manners, sharing with others, kindness, cooperation, teamwork, and empathy. In the cognitive area, parents are generally the first adults to teach children such things as colors, the alphabet, words, animals, foods, dangerous objects, and numbers. Parents are usually the first to teach their children how to walk, talk, ride a bicycle, ride a sled, read, and play sports. In general, parents are highly involved in the teaching of multiple skills to their children long before the children enter school. The formative years from ages one to four make up the period when tremendous learning and development are taking place in the lives of young children. That is the period of time when the children are usually under the care of their first teachers, their parents.

Schools have taken on the charge of providing training and development opportunities for parents. As partners in the education of children, parents and schools are beginning to plan meaningful learning modules targeted for parents. The rationale undergirding much of the new focus on parents includes these concepts: 1) Parents are cooperative members in the educational process, 2) Two-way communication between home and school is necessary, and 3) Parents knowledgeable about the curriculum can be of help to and an extension of the school. The No Child Left Behind Act is forcing states to establish specific benchmarks and student achievement levels in the core academic areas for schools. The schools that have not done so in the past are now realizing that parents can be most helpful in the process of helping students meet current achievement expectations.

In the United States, children usually enter kindergarten at age five and first grade at age six. In some areas of the country, many students begin their formal education at age four in schools that offer pre-kindergarten programs. Many students participate in Head Start programs during their early years. Recent trends have shown that some parents have relegated a great degree of the educational training of their children in the formative years to instruction offered at daycare centers. Many childcare centers provide care for children starting at the baby stage.

In our society, schools are generally expected to provide formal education to the students in their area. Attendance zones are drawn in nearly every school district, and students are given the opportunity to attend the schools within the zone in which they live. In some areas, parents have the option of sending their children to schools outside of the school attendance zone in which they live. Most students in the country attend schools in the zones organized for the area in which they reside. In recent years, however, many parents have decided to enroll their children in charter schools, private schools, and parochial schools for a variety of reasons. Some parents have participated in voucher programs that allow them to enroll their children in parochial and private schools where permitted by law. It should also be noted that a growing number of parents have elected to homeschool their children.

Once the children have been enrolled in public, charter, private, or parochial schools, they follow the curriculum of the schools. Once enrolled, students become the captive audience of the curriculum and the adults hired to deliver the curriculum. Students who are attending schools with excellent teaching and proper instructional supplies and equipment seem to have a better chance of excelling. Likewise, students who have strong support from parents in their learning endeavors seem to achieve at high levels. Student achievement improves greatly when parents know and support the school mission, are visible in the school on a regular basis, offer suggestions for school improvement, volunteer to serve on various school committees, plan supportive activities for the school, know and reinforce school rules, ensure attendance, promote excellence, teach proper study habits, provide reading materials, provide a place to study, and promote high expectations for achievement. Working together, adults/parents in the homes and adults in the schools foster high student achievement when positive home/school relations exist. Thus, a positive home/school relationship is a key characteristic of a school that is effective for students.

Many schools and school districts are trying to increase the involvement of parents in the education of their children. It is common, especially in many urban areas, for teachers and administrators to complain about the low level of parent participation in the educational process. It is also quite common to hear parents expressing complaints about not being welcomed

3

at schools and being omitted from the educational process. In some communities with low socio-economic conditions, parents are working two and three jobs and thus have little time for major involvement in the schools that their children attend. In other areas, both mothers and fathers are working long hours in order to generate sufficient income to cover living expenses that come about in middle class living.

In recent years, many novel plans have been organized to educate school leaders and parents about different types of parent involvement in schools. As the superintendent in the Buffalo Public Schools, I had the fortunate experience of introducing the dynamic parent involvement model organized and advocated by Joyce Epstein — commonly known as the Epstein Model. The Epstein Model identified the following six important types of cooperation among families, schools, and community organizations necessary to benefit schools and student learning:

Parenting: Parents and schools work together to help all families establish positive home environments to support children as student learners.

Communicating: Parents and schools work together to form school-to-home and home-to-school communications about school curriculum, programs and children's progress.

Volunteering: Structure plans to recruit and organize parent help, support and involvement in schools.

Learning at Home: Schools to provide information and suggestions to families about helping students at home with their homework and other school related learning activities.

Decision Making: Structure plans for the inclusion of parents in school decisions and the development of parent leaders and representatives.

Collaborating with Community: Structure plans to identify and integrate resources and services from the community to strengthen student learning, student development, family practices, and school programs.[1]

My experiences with fully implementing the Epstein Model have been highly successful. I found that it provided one or more avenues for parents to get involved in schools based on their interests.

The goal of schools is to foster mastery of the curriculum. The challenges to most schools center around the delivery of the curriculum to all students and involving parents in the process. It is one thing to have a written curriculum that is properly mapped out. It is another thing to have all students master the curriculum. Staff development and parent training seem to be key factors in the complex charge of providing high quality education to all children. Staff development and training are considered by many people as being synonymous. In this project, the meaning of the two will be considered the same. First, let us focus on staff development.

Most corporations allocate significant funds annually for staff development. Staff development is considered by many organizations as being key to remaining current and planning for the future. Possessing structured programs for staff development fosters security and results in the corporate world. In education, the same concepts hold true because educators are expected to deliver the curriculum to all students.

It has become clear that educators must participate in ongoing, structured and meaningful development in the profession. Educators must keep up with the times. In their book, *Professional Learning Communities at Work*, the nationally renowned educators Richard DuFour and Robert Eaker suggest that schools must become learning communities with ongoing training for employees. They write further that "The most promising strategy for sustained, substantive school improvement is developing the ability of school personnel to function as professional learning communities."[2]

It is interesting to note that, even though the fundamentals of teaching remain constant, there are critical elements supporting the process of teaching that require new skills from present-day teachers. Keep in mind that the expectations for teaching have changed dramatically during the past seventy years. In earlier times, teachers taught using, basically, books and chalkboards. In earlier times, teachers did not have such teaching aids as computers, Palm Pilots™, instructional software, distance learning, web pages, DVDs, CDs, digital cameras, PowerPoint™, virtual classrooms, and other technologies. The area of technology alone has caused many school districts to encourage, and in some cases, to mandate structured staff development in that specific area. Why? Because a large number of veteran teachers received their teaching credentials and college training before much of the present-day technologies were developed and readily available.

Today, nearly all teachers are providing instruction to students who have grown up using computers and other technologies. Teachers and others in the profession of education are now expected to grow with the times by developing their skills in the field of technology and other areas. It should be noted that, even though major focus is now being placed on the training of educators in the areas of technology, there are many other areas emerging in the profession that require and demand attention for staff development. Some of the areas in which many teachers and other educators are trained include the following areas:

Organize and Implement Staff and
Parent Development Programs

- Bilingual education
- Special education
- Differentiation strategies for classroom instruction
- Cooperative learning
- Cooperative discipline
- Looping
- Team teaching
- Authentic instruction
- Gifted education
- Phonics
- Guided reading
- Reading recovery
- Everyday mathematics
- Applied math
- Authentic assessment
- Writing processes
- Writing across the curriculum
- Reading across the curriculum
- Listening skills
- Instructional pacing
- Technology instruction

The area of staff development today is expansive. School districts are taking special care in selecting the areas of staff development that will benefit their employees based on the needs of the students. Many districts are developing structured staff development programs after reviewing student test results and teacher evaluations.

For parents, in many schools there are emerging substantive parent development and training classes in such areas as:

- Curriculum content for each grade level

- Child motivation
- Nutrition
- Behavior modification
- Child discipline techniques
- State testing
- Writing process
- Authentic assessment
- Language arts
- Bilingual education
- Cooking
- Computer skills and software
- Parent rights
- Student code of conduct
- GED
- College classes
- Mathematics
- Parenting skills

In most school districts, especially those that receive Title I funds, parent involvement and training exist to fulfill federal and state requirements. Many school districts allocate Title I dollars to provide extensive parent development seminars, workshops, courses, and other learning activities. In many areas, large parent education centers and other facilities have been established solely for use by parents in the school district. One prime example of a nationally recognized parent development center was organized by the great educator and parent leader, Howard Lewis, in Buffalo, New York. As superintendent, I had the honor of working with this great educator and parent leader who dedicated his life to providing the best opportunities possible for parents to improve their educational and parenting skills to benefit children. If there ever was an award for legendary success in leading parent involvement in education, it would have been awarded to Howard Lewis.

The key factor inherent in this concept is the idea that student achievement can be fostered when adults — be they teachers, principals or parents — receive development and training. Because parents and classroom teachers are expected to fulfill key roles in the educational process of children, it seems to follow that schools should take the necessary steps to ensure opportunities for proper staff and parent development.

3

Footnotes

[1] Joyce Epstein Model

[2] Richard DuFour and Robert Eaker, *Professional Learning Communities at Work* (Bloomington: National Educational Service, 1998), pp. xi-xii.

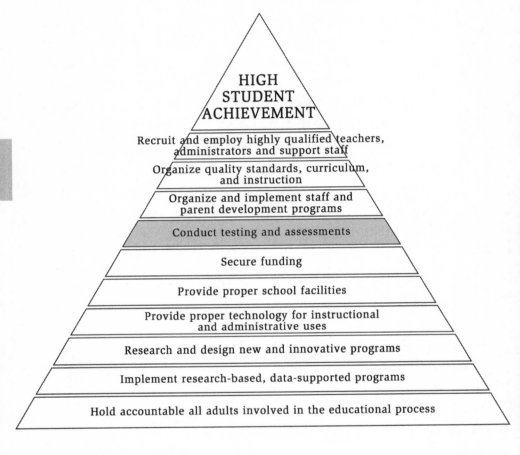

HIGH STUDENT ACHIEVEMENT

Recruit and employ highly qualified teachers, administrators and support staff

Organize quality standards, curriculum, and instruction

Organize and implement staff and parent development programs

Conduct testing and assessments

Secure funding

Provide proper school facilities

Provide proper technology for instructional and administrative uses

Research and design new and innovative programs

Implement research-based, data-supported programs

Hold accountable all adults involved in the educational process

Ten essential strategies for adults
supporting high student achievement.

STRATEGY NUMBER FOUR:

Conduct Testing and Assessments

4

The words "test" and "assessment" often bring stress and fear into the minds of many people. Because of bad experiences in the past, many people tend to think negatively about testing and assessments related to schools. This chapter, however, presents the concept that, when organized properly by adults, testing and assessments can be of high value in the process of fostering high student achievement.

In many instances, the words "testing" and "assessment" are used synonymously. Many people tend to think and use the words without regard to their technical meanings. Even states have labeled their testing as assessments (Michigan Education Assessment Program (MEAP).

The *Merriam-Webster Dictionary* defines a test as "a critical examination or evaluation."[1] In the field of education, the definitions of the two words are taken seriously by scholars interested in clarifying their meanings.

Grant Wiggins in his book, *Assessing Student Performance*, writes with great interest about the meaning of the two words. In describing testing, he writes the following: "An educational test . . . is an instrument, a measuring device. We construct an event to yield a measurement"[2] (p. 13). Writing about assessment, he suggests that "an assessment is a comprehensive, multi-faceted analysis of performance; it must be judgment-based and personal"[3] (p. 13).

A more detailed exploration of testing that takes place in schools today is most interesting. Some people believe that students are involved in too much testing today. Some believe that students spend too much time being prepared for various tests at the expense of general instructional activities. Depending on the district involved, students can be involved in testing annually for as many three to five days or more.

4

There are basically two types of tests in the field of education: *norm-referenced tests* and *criterion-referenced tests.*[4] Norm-referenced tests are used to compare students with others in the reference group. For example, norm-referenced test results might be used to compare fourth-graders throughout the United States and Canada. The criterion-referenced tests results are compared to criteria established by a teacher to determine progress (e.g., twenty words defined correctly each week). The criterion-referenced tests basically compare individuals, not to each other, but to expected levels of performance.

Over the years, the field of psychometry has become highly specialized. A myriad of testing and assessment types have been developed by psychometricians to serve the various needs of students in schools today.

An interesting aspect of testing that is often discussed has to do with validity and reliability. A test is valid if it tests the things for which it was designed.[5] For example, a test with all questions on rocks could be valid in the field of geology, but not valid in the field of psychology. A test is reliable when it produces similar results from students when given multiple times.[6]

The important factors related to testing and assessments have to do with the respective responsibilities of students and adults. The adults in the majority of the cases in education develop and administer tests and assessments. Students make up the captive audience, a role that requires them to participate in the tests and assessments. The students are the ones that are often looked upon as having been successes or failures on the instruments developed by the adults. As participants, the students are at the mercy of the adults who organize tests and assessments. In general, students do not have the experience and know-how to determine if tests that have been designed by adult designers are valid and reliable. Students only know that they are required to take the tests presented to them.

Unfortunately, many students have had to take tests that were laced with errors. In some cases, the errors were eventually observed. However, in many cases, the errors were not observed and the students, unbeknownst to them, had to take the bad tests. In cases where students have been required to take error-laced tests, the students were often labeled as having performed poorly. In such cases, the true poor performers were the adults for having developed tests with errors.

The important concept being presented in this chapter is that testing and assessment instruments must be designed and used properly in order to foster high student achievement. Tests and assessments that are improperly organized can do harm to students by presenting incorrect scores and information. Students are highly impressionable during their school-age years. Thus, adults must take proper care to ensure accuracy, validity, and reliability when testing and assessing the educational aspects of students and programs that purport to help students.

A special aspect of testing and assessment relates to how these instruments can be used to improve student achievement. Practitioners in the field of education rely heavily on the results of tests and assessments. Properly constructed and used, test and assessment results can be used for the following:

4

- Diagnostic planning
- Remediation
- Academic placement
- Intervention
- Analysis of student knowledge
- Effectiveness of instructional programs
- Comparisons in norm groups

A plethora of positive rationales exist for the proper use of tests and assessments in the process of improving student achievement. It seems to make sense for all in the educational process to use data, especially test data, to help in determining and organizing programs that will lead to improving student achievement.

Data-driven educational actions can be highly justified. Educational programs organized based on speculations and hunches can often be inefficient and harmful to all in the process — students and adults. Testing and assessment processes, by their very nature, produce data vital in the educational process.

When an individual goes to the doctor, it is the routine of the doctor to conduct a series of tests and an interview before prescribing corrective medical or physical intervention. A qualified doctor takes time to read the data on the patient and to consider possible options before making recommendations for the next steps. An individual should suspect a doctor of being a sham when corrective actions are prescribed without proper testing.

The field of education is now enduring contrasting arguments and research related to the importance of testing and assessments designed to improve student achievement. On one side, a strong argument suggests that a large amount of testing only detracts from the goal of educating children. That argument suggests further that testing takes too much valuable time away from teaching. Embedded in this argument is the idea that testing should be held to a very limited level. This argument suggests that, when students are allowed to pursue their interests, they will achieve at levels aligned to their abilities. This argument holds that human beings will naturally achieve at certain levels regardless of the efforts to tease out their present academic levels. This technical concept is rooted in the notion of IQ being set with little possible fluxion. Fortunately, this concept has been countered by other strong bodies of research.

On the other side, a strong argument exists suggesting that testing and assessments have value related to fostering student achievement and accountability. Considered by some as a business model, the concept calls for one to garner as much information as possible at the beginning of an educational process in order to make wise decisions in planning. In other words, use data to plan and make decisions in education, just like good doctors use data in medical processes. Test students and assess programs in order to foster results. Of course, the critical drivers in this concept are the adults empowered to make the decisions that impact students in schools all across the country. When adults do their jobs properly, students will achieve at high levels.

Footnotes

[1] *Merriam-Webster Dictionary* (Springfield: Merriam-Webster, 1997).

[2] Grant Wiggins, *Assessing Student Performance* (San Francisco: Jossey-Bass Publishers, 1993), 13.

[3] Ibid., 13.

[4] Gilbert Sax, *Principles of Educational Measurement and Evaluation* (Belmont, CA: Wadesworth Publishing Company, 1974), 8.

[5] Ibid., 205.

[6] Ibid., 172.

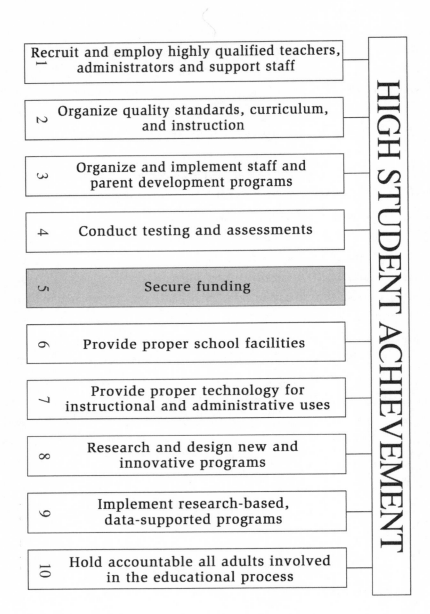

1	Recruit and employ highly qualified teachers, administrators and support staff
2	Organize quality standards, curriculum, and instruction
3	Organize and implement staff and parent development programs
4	Conduct testing and assessments
5	Secure funding
6	Provide proper school facilities
7	Provide proper technology for instructional and administrative uses
8	Research and design new and innovative programs
9	Implement research-based, data-supported programs
10	Hold accountable all adults involved in the educational process

HIGH STUDENT ACHIEVEMENT

5

Ten essential strategies for adults
supporting high student achievement.

STRATEGY NUMBER FIVE:

Secure Funding to
Improve Student Achievement

Up to this point, it has been presented that adults are the driving factors in fostering high student achievement. Adults do the hiring of employees in a school district. Adults write the curriculum that students are expected to learn. Adults do the teaching and supervision. Adults serve as the parents and guardians of students. Adults do the testing and assessments of students and programs. The concept is beginning to take root that student achievement is largely dependent upon the quality of work done by adults. In this chapter, focus will be placed on a vital educational pillar provided primarily by adults — funding for education.

Historically, the majority of parents and civic-minded adults have supported the idea of providing education and schools for children to learn core academic skills — reading, writing, mathematics — and other worthwhile knowledge. In the United States, early farmers pooled their dollars and crops to fund the hiring of a person, usually an unmarried woman, to teach their children the three Rs ("readin', writin', 'rithmetic"). All across the country there existed one and two room schoolhouses in the early days, schools funded by local people. In cities, the prominent leaders usually served on school boards organized to pro-

5

vide leadership in the funding of schools for students. Over a period of time, states and even the federal government became involved in the funding of the education of students.

Official reports from the early days of schools in our country showed how various states were organized to fund education. For example, on January 15, 1845, the Superintendent of Common Schools in the state of New York provided the following insights into the enormity of education during that period in his report to the State of New York Assembly:

> The entire territory of the State, comprising, exclusively of the waters of the Great Lakes, an area of 45,658 square miles, has been subdivided into 10,990 school districts, averaging somewhat more than four square miles each — seldom, especially in the rural districts, varying essentially from this average — and bringing the remotest inhabitants of the respective districts within a little more than one mile of the school house.
>
> Every male person of full age, residing in any school district, and entitled to hold lands in this State (including aliens who have filed their certificate of intention to become citizens, in the mode prescribed by law,) who owns or hire real property in Such district, subject to taxation for school purposes, and every resident of such district authorized to vote at town meetings, who has paid a rate bill for teacher's wages therein within one year, or a tax for district purposes within two years preceding, or who possesses personal property liable to taxation for school purposes, exceeding fifty dollars in value, beyond such as is exempt from execution, is entitled to vote at school district meetings, for the choice of officers of the

5

district, and upon any question which may properly come before such meetings.

Under the act of 1843, three trustees were chosen in that year, in each district, for one, two, and three years respectively; and in each succeeding year, one trustee is annually to be chosen by the inhabitants and legal voters, who, in conjunction with his colleagues previously chosen, holds his office for three years. Each district also annually chooses a clerk, collector and librarian. The inhabitants have power, whenever lawfully assembled to designate one or more sites for the district school house; to lay such tax on the taxable inhabitants of the district, as may be deemed necessary to purchase or lease such sites, and to build, hire, or purchase a school house, or houses, and to keep in repair and furnish the same with necessary fuel and appendages, and generally to transact such other business as the interests of the district organization may require.[1]

Think of it for a moment: 10,990 school districts were in the state of New York in 1845. Think further about the number of people involved and the complexities of collecting taxes to fund schools of that period.

The model for funding schools in the state of New York in the early days was copied by many other states. From those early days to the present, funding of schools has been a challenge and a topic for discussion.

School finance has been and remains a pillar of imperative in proving and improving student achievement. No matter how experts slice and dice the research, the fact is that the funding of education remains one of the centrist elements in the process of education. It takes funding to hire good teachers, administrators and other staff. With the advent of unions and other associations, no longer will people work for low wages in the field of education. In fact, the formula for operating schools is constant — 80 to 85 percent for salaries (teachers, administrators, and other staff), and the rest (15 to 20 percent) for all other costs (books, equipment, utilities, buses, building repairs, and staff development). Today, when people work, they expect to be paid. Thus, for schools to be operated, there must be funds provided.

On the various levels, courts have gotten involved in issues related to financing schools in the country. Arguments have been presented to various courts highlighting the following:

1. Protection provided by the equal-protection clause of the Fourteenth Amendment to the Constitution of the United States (No State shall…deny to any person within its jurisdiction the equal protection of the laws).

2. Equal-protection clause interpretation by the Supreme Court in the *Brown v. Board of Education* case (The opportunity of an education, . . . where the state has undertaken to provide it, is a right which must be made available to all on equal terms).[2]

Pivotal cases resulted in the early decisions and interventions from the courts into the morass of funding for schools. On August 30, 1971, the California Supreme Court in the *Serrano v. Priest* case decided that the "state's public school financing system is unconstitutional."[3] Sometime later in the *Van Dusartz v. Hatfield* case in Minnesota, a federal court reached a similar decision about school funding.[4] In a similar decision, a three-judge federal district court in Texas ruled that the state's system of financing schools was unconstitutional in the verdict rendered in the *Rodriguez v. San Antonio School District* case.[5]

Secure Funding to Improve
Student Achievement

The states of Kentucky, New Jersey, New York, Texas, California and others have witnessed judicial decisions rendered to foster school funding related to improving equity, quantity, desegregation and quality in education.

Traditionally, in the United States, funds for schools have been provided from the following sources:

Property Taxes. Over time, it has been proven that property taxes are the most reliable source for funding education. On the positive side, the property owners in the school district are required to support education by paying an amount based on the value of their property holdings. This funding model usually provides a funding base that a school district can count on. On the negative side, property owners often grouse at having to pay ever-increasing taxes to fund schools.

Partnerships, Foundations, Tuitions, Gifts. Many school districts have organized special partnerships with businesses, universities and community groups to provide general and special funding. Foundations have been organized to raise funds to provide financial support to various aspects of school districts. Many districts have organized district and individual school booster clubs and parent/teacher organizations (PTO) to raise funds. Many districts advertise and collect tuition from students who qualify for paying due to the jurisdiction in which they live.

State and Federal General Operating Funds. In some areas of the country, school districts have been, and remain, funded in part or in full by the state or the federal government. The state and federal funding of schools, in full or in part, is usually associated with such circumstances as school districts in large urban areas, thinly populated rural areas, military bases, reservations, and experimental projects. For example, the "Big Five" school districts in the state of New York (New York City, Buffalo, Rochester, Syracuse, and Yonkers) receive more than half of their annual funding from the state. In the case of Buffalo, the state provides approximately 80 percent of the funding annually. Since educating students is ultimately the responsibility of the individual states, the record shows that many school districts, especially those districts with very low property bases and low socio-economic conditions receive funding assistance. Annually, the National Association of Federally Impacted Schools (NAFIS) provides updates on the funding provided by the federal government for schools on military bases in this country and in other countries.

5

State and Federal Grants. Following are the three types of state and federal grants:

- *Competitive grants.* These grants are awarded based on proposals and applications submitted. Each state and the federal government provide listings of the various competitive grants available to school districts. Information on the grants is often available on the website links related to grants.
- *Direct grants.* These are grants that are awarded to school districts directly. Various conditions might justify the awarding of these grants. Often, school districts are awarded these direct grants based on socio-economic conditions, political connections, need, student achievement, special programs, and many other factors.
- *Entitlement grants.* The largest number of dollars usually given to school districts are in the forms of entitlement grants. These are grants that schools in the districts are entitled to receive because they meet the requirements of the grants. The word "entitlement" is very important for

these grants because conditions in certain schools make them eligible for the entitlement grants. Following is a listing of the most prominent entitlement grants:*

- *Title I.* This grant is designed to help disadvantaged students meet high standards. Schools design their own programs with parental input to foster improvements.

- *Title II Part A.* This grant is used to prepare, train, and recruit high quality-teachers, principals and paraprofessionals. The grant is also used for class-size reduction.

- *Title II Part D.* This grant is used to enhance education through technology.

- *Title V.* This grant provides funds for curriculum development, new and innovative programs.

- *Title IV.* This grant is used to maintain and develop effective research-based strategies targeted toward drug and violence prevention in schools.

5

It goes without saying that all of the various grants are designed ultimately to foster improvement in student achievement. Further, all of the grants are organized and administered not by students but by adults. The quality of the design, implementation, and administration of the grants often reflects their impact on student achievement. Grants that are poorly designed, poorly implemented, and poorly administered often have weak impact on students. In some cases, unfortunately, the adults reap greater benefits — jobs — from grants than the students.

Earlier, the idea was presented relative to property taxes being the most reliable and popular form of funding for schools. There have, however, been exceptions and alternate models for funding schools. A notable alternate funding model has been used in the State of Michigan. The model was implemented in 1995 under the guidelines of Proposal A. The essence of the Michigan education-funding model called for an increase of 2 percent in the sales tax to be used to fund education in combination with funds from the lottery, businesses, and a very small amount from property owners forwarded directly to the state. All of the funds, including the lion's share from the 2 percent sales tax, have been combined to provide the funding for education in Michigan.

The Michigan education funding plan was hailed as innovative by many people in 1995, especially the property owners. Accompanying the implementation of the 1995 Michigan education-funding plan (Proposal A), however, was a warning from some school finance experts that the state's dependency on the 2 percent sales tax to fund education would work well during good economic times and poorly during weak economic times. As predicted, the plan worked well from 1995 to 2000, with strong economic conditions in the country and the state. The plan turned sour when the economy in the state became bad starting in late 2000. Michigan, California, New York, and a host of other states were hit hard by the major downturn of the stock market, the Silicon Valley bust, the energy crisis and the increase in unemployment. Michigan witnessed escalating costs for education with a corresponding declining sales tax base for funding education. In Michigan, people had less money to spend due to the declining economy. What suffered? The Education Fund in Michigan. Who suffered most? Students in many schools, because the schools had to make reductions in order to keep their budgets balanced. In Michigan, the state comes in and takes over the operation of a school district that is

Secure Funding to Improve
Student Achievement

unable to operate with a balanced budget, for example, the Inkster School District.

As a superintendent in a school district in California (Inglewood) and later in Michigan (Taylor), I witnessed first-hand the funding issues in both states. In California, the energy and Silicon Valley problems were monumental to the budget of the state. Schools suffered because the economy of the state was down.

The most dramatic funding situation that I endured as a superintendent, however, was in Michigan during the period 2002 to 2004 when the state took funds back from all school districts mid-year — proration. How does one operate a school district when the funds are cut mid-year? It takes creative planning, collaborative unions, understanding employees, and good internal and external communications. In our case, nearly $900,000 was subtracted from our allocation from the state mid-year. Fortunately, based on the mid-year takeback from the previous year, we had placed funds in the budget to cover the anticipated takeback. Such actions on our part fostered a balanced budget. Such action also brought on the layoff of over forty employees, elimination of bus transportation for high school students, implementation of a $70 pay-to-participate fee per sport for students, alternate day cleaning of some classrooms, increases in class sizes, and the selling of certain district owned properties. Ultimately, who suffered from such actions? Students.

School finance in the twenty-first century is interesting, complex and ever-changing. As a critical element driving education, funding for schools remains controversial, insufficient and in need of reform. Schools are being mandated to meet the requirements imposed by states and the federal government under the No Child Left Behind Act of 2001. The funding

5

requirements for quality employees, health care, pension/retirement, building repairs, utilities, technology, and the cost of living are increasing concurrently. So what is the long-term answer to the perplexing question of school funding to improve student achievement in the United States?

Of course, there have been many scholarly articles and books written on the topic of school finance that attempt to deal with the perplexing issue of providing proper funding to spur and foster high student achievement. Much of the data now available seem to show that in nearly all cases, schools in high socio-economic communities have higher test scores and other educational amenities than those in low socio-economic communities. In other words, schools with high per-pupil expenditure tend to produce much higher student achievement levels than those schools with low per-pupil expenditure.

As a superintendent, I would often josh with superintendents, principals, and teachers from high per-pupil funded districts by asking each to give up his or her present assignment and move into an assignment in a district with low per-pupil funding. After more than two decades of offering the exchange opportunities, no one has taken the offer. Why? For obvious reasons, it is well known in the educational arena that it is essential to have proper funding in order to provide students with proper educational instruction, staffing, equipment, facilities, field trips, and supplies. One person even expressed to me that he would not want to go into battle without the proper funding, supplies, equipment, staff, and plans. He suggested that he preferred remaining in his school district with high per-pupil funding support because the district was producing students with the highest test scores in the state. He stated further that it would be totally unfair to expect his students to perform at high levels if his school did not have all of the proper instructional materials, supplies, equipment, facilities, and other support necessary for him to be effective as a teacher.

The reality of life in the field of education shows that there are "have" and "have-not" schools in the United States. Yet, the "have-nots" are being expected to be on par with the "haves" in the area of student achievement as mandated by the No Child Left Behind Act of 2001. The act mandates that all students are to be proficient in the core academic areas by the year 2014. The objective is laudable. However, the funding means for achieving the objective is being questioned by many people, especially educators in districts that are in low socio-economic areas, rural and otherwise.

In order to face and resolve the school funding issue directly, I recommend that the following menu of steps be taken:

1. States declare in legislation that all schools will be funded using a weighted formula.
2. A base/floor per-pupil funding level would be established to serve as the foundation for the weighted funding allocation that would be built.
3. Schools would be funded based on property taxes and other funding sources.
4. A national initiative will be implemented to fund the infrastructure of schools across the country. The concept is analogous to the implementation of the Marshall Plan after World II. The concept is also similar to the plan designed and initiated by President Eisenhower to build interstate superhighways across the country. It was deemed by the president at that time that such action was in the national interest of the country. Providing the proper funds to rebuild the educational infrastructure/school buildings of this country is similarly in the national interest of the country. The

foundation of every country is the education of its youth and all citizens. It should be of interest that, since 1997, the Council of Great City Schools has been advocating a dynamic Marshall Plan for improving urban schools and student achievement for many years. The CGCS Marshall Plan is rooted in the concepts inspired by former U.S. Supreme Court Justice Thurgood Marshall. The CGCS plan calls for the following to be done to improve schools and student achievement, especially in urban schools:

(a) Set high expectations for all students. Schools to establish and implement rigorous academic content and performance standards for all students with aligned curriculum, instructional practices and assessments.

(b) Provide well-trained teachers and staff.

(c) Provide schools with the programs and tools they need to increase achievement.

(d) Strengthen school system leadership, management and administration, and enhance school decision-making.

(e) Design assessment systems that hold everyone accountable for results.

(f) Seek adequate resources and ensure that they are used effectively and efficiently.

(g) Build public support for the education of urban children.

(h) Link schools and students with the community supports and social services they need to succeed.

5. Funding of entitlement grants. The concepts presented here are rooted in the idea that all children can learn when adults do their work properly. Conversely, the concepts imply that it is folly to expect all students to achieve at high levels when adults fail to do their jobs properly. High achievement by students is impacted negatively when there is improper

Secure Funding to Improve
Student Achievement

funding by adults for schools; when students have to sit daily in school buildings that are leaking, drafty, too hot or too cold, provided for them by adults; when they have unqualified teachers and administrators as provided for them by adults; or when they are taught a curriculum, provided by adults, that does not prepare them for college or the world of work. There must be checks and balances in the entire educational process in order to foster efficient use of funds and other resources in order to foster high student achievement.

Footnotes

[1] Annual Report of the Superintendent of Common Schools of the State of New York (Michigan Assembly, 1845), 3.

[2] Arthur Wise, *Rich Schools, Poor Schools* (Chicago: University of Chicago Press, 1972), 7.

[3] Ibid., xii.

[4] Ibid., xii.

[5] Ibid., xiv.

5

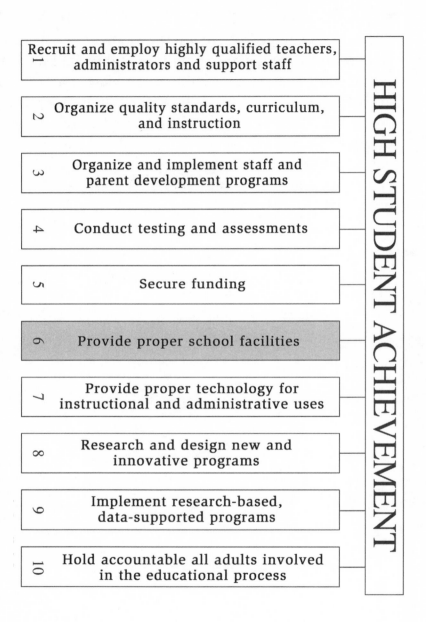

1	Recruit and employ highly qualified teachers, administrators and support staff
2	Organize quality standards, curriculum, and instruction
3	Organize and implement staff and parent development programs
4	Conduct testing and assessments
5	Secure funding
6	Provide proper school facilities
7	Provide proper technology for instructional and administrative uses
8	Research and design new and innovative programs
9	Implement research-based, data-supported programs
10	Hold accountable all adults involved in the educational process

HIGH STUDENT ACHIEVEMENT

6

Ten essential strategies for adults supporting high student achievement.

STRATEGY NUMBER SIX:

Provide Proper School Facilities
for Students

A major element in the total process of fostering high student achievement has to do with school facilities. In this context, school facilities will encompass all of the physical buildings, classrooms, science laboratories, workrooms, grounds, physical education facilities, athletic and marching band fields, and all other areas pertinent to providing education to students. Just as the elements presented in the preceding chapters have been highlighted as important, so too are the elements of school facilities.

There are many fundamental areas that can be suggested as being critical to fostering success in educating students. The argument is often presented that such areas as curriculum, personnel, funding, and testing are far more important than school facilities. Contrary to the tenets of that argument, a strong series of ideas exists supporting the notion that school facilities rank high in the complex order of providing quality education to students. The process of education requires the following five fundamental pillars to be in place in order to foster strategies for high student achievement:

1. Personnel Component
2. Curriculum and Instruction

6

3. Business/Finance/Budget
4. Facilities/Support Services
5. Communications/Community Relations

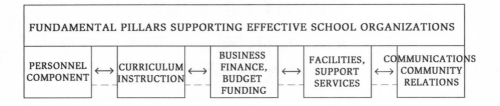

Based on volumes of research and decades as an educational leader, I am convinced that the above fundamental pillars are vital to the success of all schools and school districts. Weakness in any one area will greatly diminish the effectiveness of the organization.

Focusing on the area of facilities is fascinating because it causes one to reflect on the importance of proper facilities in the educational process. In this era of modern facilities in our society, pressure is mounting for school districts to upgrade and to build new facilities, ones more along the mall concept. Students today enjoy spending time at the malls with their friends because the malls are inviting places to be. The malls are cheerful, bright, spacious, inviting, colorful and contemporary. The malls cater to the interests of the customers in order to attract sales and to increase foot traffic. In many areas, suburban shopping malls caused the demise of many downtown shopping areas. For example, in the city of Detroit, the downtown area has witnessed a major flight of stores out of the city as the building of suburban malls has increased.* The new malls usually provide such amenities as comfort, climate control, free parking, stores in close proximity to each other, and a safe environment. Thus, people of all ages tend to enjoy going to the mall, especially students.

Provide Proper School Facilities
for Students

The mall concept is being included in this section for a specific reason. It is now clear that in order for schools of the future to foster high student achievement, many of the mall attributes must be infused into schools. School facilities must be brought up to contemporary standards in order to attract students and adults and in order to be effective. That is, the "foot traffic" in schools must be improved.

Historically, the majority of the school buildings in the United States were built during the period from 1945 to 1975. After World War II and the Korean War, the United States witnessed the Baby Boom and a rapid school-building response period for nearly three decades. In nearly every community, schools were built reflecting the standards of that period — a pre-information age, pre-technology period. In general, school buildings of the 1900s were designed to serve students in two basic categories — college preparatory and vocational. Early classrooms were not built to house the plethora of programs that have emerged during the latter decades of the 1900s and early 2000s. In the area of special education alone, the school buildings from the mid-1950s period have been deemed inadequate to house all of the space needed by now-required support staff (psychologists, speech therapists, social workers, counselors, and resource rooms). As a federal mandate, special education became a vital part of the educational process in schools with the enactment of the Education of All Handicapped Children Act of 1975, P.L. 94-142. The act was amended in 1990 and 1991 with a name change to the Individuals with Disabilities Act (IDEA). Unfortunately, most school buildings have not been renovated to meet the proper needs of students with disabilities.

The entire need for new and improved school facilities is so massive that it can boggle the mind. In a report entitled

6

"Modernizing Our Schools: What Will it Cost?" the National Education Association projected that the total funding needed would be $321.9 billion ($268.2 billion for infrastructure and $53.7 billion for educational technologies).[1] In many communities, especially in low socio-economic areas, students are attending schools that are leaking, drafty, drab, cold in the winter and hot in the summer and, in general, uninviting. A large number of students in the country spend seven to eight hours a day, five days a week, 180 days a year, in school buildings that most adults would not tolerate being in for even a week.

Jonathan Kozol depicts in his book, *Savage Inequalities*, the bleak conditions that he saw firsthand in school districts all across the United States, particularly in large, urban areas.[2] The book presented descriptions of conditions that shocked the sensitivities of many people around the country, and received national attention. Unfortunately, the conditions in many school buildings remain deplorable decades after the publishing of *Savage Inequalities*. Teachers, school psychologists, social workers, librarians, and other employees are still working with students in areas that many professionals deem unsuitable for educational activities. Unfortunately, in many schools that I have seen, it is still common to see buckets in hallways and in classrooms with students on rainy days to catch water leaking into the schools. Many schools have not been painted inside since they were built. One could say that such conditions should not exist in the United States today. The reality is that, unfortunately, such conditions do exist at alarming levels. The school buildings in the United States are in need of immediate attention for improvements.

As a school superintendent, I have visited over five hundred schools in the southern, western, eastern and northern parts of the United States. I had the wonderful opportunities to serve as

Provide Proper School Facilities
for Students

superintendent in school districts located in the Midwest (Michigan, Illinois), the North (New York), and the West (California). As an undergraduate student, I had the opportunity to study at Virginia State University in the State of Virginia (the South). So I have observed schools in nearly every section of the country. The vast amount of school observations and work experiences all over the United State that I have had support the notion that a very large number of school buildings in the country are in desperate need of repair, renovations, and upgrading. Also, there are large numbers of school buildings that simply need be demolished and rebuilt. There are school buildings that are actually hurting students daily because of poorly contained asbestos, rust- or lead-filled drinking water, improper heating, improper ventilation, poor lighting, unsanitary restroom facilities, old desks and chairs, unsafe science labs, and unsafe storage of chemicals. Believe it or not, such conditions exist today in many schools — not as the exception, but as the rule of reality. Working with various boards of education, I, along with hundreds of other superintendents, have taken the baton with the commitment to improve student achievement by improving the conditions of the school facilities.

Our surroundings and our environment impact many parts of our lives. Our mental and physical states are influenced by things around us daily. Many people know the exhilarating feeling of owning and driving a new car or owning a new home. Many people know the pride that comes with completing and enjoying repairs and renovations made in facilities. Believe it or not, students have the same feelings of pride, exhilaration, confidence, and even excitement associated with new and properly designed facilities. Schools can be as inviting to students as the malls with proper planning and funding.

6

Education for the twenty-first century will require that school facilities be renovated and, in many cases, rebuilt to meet the needs of students. The critical issue is paying for the needed facility changes. Taxpayers in many school districts are refusing to pass bonds to repair and rebuild school facilities. The general fund of many school districts cannot pay for the vast amount of repairs that are needed. Yet, the mandate from No Child Left Behind is to improve student achievement by having all students proficient by 2014. The irony in education is that many schools are being asked to achieve high standards in substandard facilities. Can we really have students achieve at high levels in science when there are not properly functioning science labs in schools? The humorous analogy is often presented where the principal is directed to "Fly this school plane that has only one wing, a few missing tires, little fuel, a faulty compass, a few missing stewards, and broken passenger seats. We expect highly pleased passengers and for you to have a safe takeoff and landing each time." The analogy captures the reality that exists in a large number of schools today. The needs are real. It boils down again to adults needing to find ways to properly fund proper school facilities. Students do not have the resources to repair, renovate and build new schools. School facilities are in the purview of adults.

Thus, to foster high school achievement, adults must shoulder their responsibility for providing students with good educational facilities.

Footnotes

[1]National Education Association, "Modernizing Our Schools: What Will it Cost?" (Washington, D.C.: National Education Association, 2000), P. 1.

[2]Jonathan Kozol, *Savage Inequalities* (New York: Crown Publishers, 1991), 1-231.

HIGH STUDENT ACHIEVEMENT

1	2	3	4	5	6	7	8	9	10
Recruit and employ highly qualified teachers, administrators and support staff	Organize quality standards, curriculum, and instruction	Organize and implement staff and parent development programs	Conduct testing and assessments	Secure funding	Provide proper school facilities	Provide proper technology for instructional and administrative uses	Research and design new and innovative programs	Implement research-based, data-supported programs	Hold accountable all adults involved in the educational process

Ten essential strategies for adults
supporting high student achievement.

7

STRATEGY NUMBER SEVEN:

Provide Proper Technology for Instructional and Administrative Uses

The cultural progression in the United States has moved from the agrarian to the industrial to the information age. Under the broad name of technology, our culture has joined most of the world in infusing technology into our daily lives. It is often suggested by many knowledgeable people that information doubles at a rapid rate — some suggest every two years. The Internet has linked most of the world with instant information and communication. Computers of various sizes and capacities are commonplace in our society. Cellphones are in use all over the world. Technology is all around us. Information on nearly all subjects is now at our fingertips via the World Wide Web. Technology today helps us access, manipulate, manage, store and use the vast amount of information now in existence. Students today have a vast reservoir of information available to them.

It is interesting to reflect on the progress that has been made in this country relative to technology on many fronts. We have progressed from the Sputnik launch in the 1950s to massive numbers of satellites in space. Satellites now provide for telecommunication, exploration, national security, warfare, information transmission, weather tracking, cellphones,

7

instruction and many others uses. We have progressed from the room-size early computers to hand-held calculators, hand-held Palm Pilots™, and hand-held computers. We have progressed from the installation of millions of miles of wires and cables to wireless and cableless computers and telephones. We have progressed using technology in the area of transportation to levels that provide the following: 1) computerized/satellite piloting of airplanes; 2) automated directions for drivers; 3) capability to track speed and location of trains, buses, trucks, and automobiles; and 4) computerized operation and monitoring of engines, tires, oil, doors, speed, traction, and climate control.

There exist thousands of examples where it can be shown that technology has progressed in our society and our individual lives. Of special interest for this chapter is the progression of technology into the area of education. Like other parts of society, the area of education has progressed with the times. I can recollect when climate control in schools referred to opening the windows in the summer and placing wood in the classroom heaters during the winters. Today, most school buildings control internal climate with sophisticated electronic controls. Today, motion- and voice-activated systems exist in some schools to control lights and security.

There are two main areas in which technology is used in schools today to improve student achievement. First, technology is now used in the area of school administration/management. Much of the administrative work that was done manually in schools of the past is now being completed using technological means. Like the progressions in the general society, the progressional use of technology in school administration has been massive and impressive. Following are some of the key administrative uses of technology currently in vogue:

7

Provide Proper Technology for
Instructional and Administrative Uses

- Budget management
- Student records
- Inventory of books, equipment, supplies, instruments
- Payroll
- Accounting
- Auditing
- Requisitioning and ordering
- Attendance for students and staff
- Substitute call-ins and assignments
- Bus routing
- Tracking of buses and other district vehicles
- Building security
- Communicating with parents, students, employees
- Recruitment and interviewing
- Employee training

Most school administrative offices look and sound different today from those of yesteryear. Whereas administrative offices of the past had manual and electric typewriters that were often loud and limited in function, the offices of today are characterized by powerful computers, printers, scanners, color copiers and many other functional pieces of technological equipment. Offices today have e-mail which allows for instantaneous transmission and reception of communications. Administrators now have the option of communicating using the traditional "hard copy" approach, or they can now use "paperless" electronic means. The bottom line is that technology allows for new and different ways for administrators to work efficiently today.

The second area of technology that is important deals with instructional technology. This concept deals with the existence and use of a wide array of technologies in the area of teaching

7

and learning. Following is a partial listing of instructional technological ideas in vogue:

- PowerPoint™
- Computer
- Palm Pilot™
- Hand-held computer
- Laptop computers
- Educational software
- Digital microscope
- Digital recording
- Computer lab
- Distance learning
- Teaching with the Web
- Animated biology
- Interactive research
- Online courses
- Online teaching
- Virtual classroom

7

Education is replete with hundreds of technologically advanced tools designed to foster higher student achievement. Today, students can go online and practice for their state tests, ACT and SAT exams and many others.

As a superintendent, I was fascinated with the interest of our students and parents in a program called Study Island. In the program, all students in elementary and secondary schools in our district were assigned a pin number that permitted them to go online to access the Study Island learning activities related to the state learning standards. The students learned skills related to the Michigan Education Assessment Program (MEAP). The parents learned how complex the MEAP items can be. It was interesting to hear comments from parents who were shocked that they could not answer most of the MEAP items. The parents thus gained greater understanding about the test. They also became sensitized to the things that their children were experiencing in education today, especially related to higher-order thinking.

As superintendent, I approved the installation of distance education classrooms in a series of high schools in our school district in order to access and implement a variety of new courses for students. The distance education design allowed our schools to offer courses that would often not be available to students because of the small number of students who would enroll in certain courses. By having one teacher teaching over the distance learning network, students from multiple schools could enroll in various courses. The distance learning teachers used technology that allowed them to see and to communicate with all of the students at the various sites simultaneously. When an individual would press a button on his or her desk, a classroom camera focused on the student and the microphone on the student's desk automatically became activated. Thus, the teachers could see and hear the students. The teachers could then press a master control button and respond. The students could always see and hear the teachers.

As a high school principal in Joliet, Illinois, I worked with my leadership team in funding the installation of a high-tech writing lab to foster the improvement of writing by students. That project was interesting in that it allowed language arts classes and other classes to participate in structured writing exercises (descriptive, expository, creative, narrative, persuasive, analytical, and others). The software reviewed the writings and provided immediate and extensive feedback related to such areas as sentence structure, paragraph structure, spelling, gram-

7

mar, punctuation, and many other areas. Students with computers at home could transmit their writings to be reviewed at any time.

In the early days of computers, the Apple Corporation provided the majority of the educational/instructional programs/software for schools, especially for elementary schools. In later years, other corporate groups began developing instructional programs. Today there exist thousands of instructional programs related to academics and testing, intended for use by schools and in homes. The qualities of the programs vary from high to weak. Many are self-paced with instant feedback. The majority of the programs are in the drill format. Today, instructional programs exist in practically all areas of learning normally found in schools (reading, mathematics, writing, speaking, science, social studies, career education, physical education, foreign languages, keyboarding, music, art, dance, and a host of others). Today, students can use the computer to access newspapers, encyclopedias, statistics, reports, magazines, journals, and other informational and reading sources. Technology has made it so convenient that many students can complete their academic assignments and other research projects without having to go to the library. They now can do research using the World Wide Web online.

In recent years, most colleges started requiring students to be computer literate. Many colleges now require students to have personal computers upon entering college. It is no longer special or unusual for students to use computers and other technologies in the areas of education. This is the age of technology and information. Computers and other technologies allow students, kindergarten to college age, to access, use, and manage the vast amount of information now available. Due to the fast doubling of information, it is understood that it has become impossible for students to memorize all of the important facts in education as traditional approaches required. Today, instructional modalities are being designed to teach students skills in accessing needed information and solving problems using contemporary technological tools and advancements.

Technology has provided new tools for teaching and learning. Just think for a moment about the resources now provided to students in schools. In a school district that I served as superintendent in California, all students in an honors high school that I organized were issued laptops for use during the school year (Inglewood, California City Honors High School). Today, students in many other schools are beginning to use hand-held computers in classrooms. In one of my school districts (Taylor, Michigan), high school students are now being issued CDs that contain the full contents of their mathematic books. The students of the school district can also access their math books via the World Wide Web. Thus, many students have multiple ways to access their learning materials. I forecast that technological advancements in the area of education will render many traditional processes and products obsolete. In the not-too-distant future, students will be issued CDs for all of their classes. The students will be issued PINs (personal identification numbers) that will allow them to access information, class syllabi, reading requirements, reading materials, class chatrooms, and sites for the depositing of class work, all online. Student lockers will have multiple class CDs instead of big bulky books. As a futurist, I foresee the days when students will have the option of attending classes at school or tuning into classes online at home, on the road or elsewhere. Believe it or not, the projections being presented here will be reality in most schools in the future — a future brought on by technology.

7

Bill Gates, in his book *Business @ the Speed of Thought,* suggests to business leaders that "How you gather, manage, and use information will determine whether you win or lose in business."[1] He further recommends in the book that leaders strive to develop a "digital nervous system" to handle the flow of information for the future.[2]

The concepts related to the field of business presented by Bill Gates in his book can be applied today to the field of education. School districts can take the "digital nervous system" concept coined by Gates and find compatible applications in education. In order to handle the massive amount of data and information in education, most school districts are in the process of seeking the means of acquiring the hardware, software, training and maintenance personnel required for the "digital nervous system." An example of a school district that has been successful in integrating technology into all levels of instruction and administration can be seen in the Naperville School District in Naperville, Illinois. It should be noted that Naperville is a high wealth school district with high student achievement annually.

The big issue present in this concept of emerging technology in education has to do with the ever-present challenge of funding in most districts. In the period of decreasing funds for education, revolting taxpayers, and increasing costs for operating schools, how can schools fund the ever-changing technologies necessary to educate students? For example, many new instructional modalities are requiring computers with more memory. Every year there are new and improved instructional technologies available, technologies with the potential of fostering improved student achievement. There are no clear and precise answers to the perplexing questions associated with school funding. Some school districts are being proactive by imple-

7

menting plans for leasing, repairing, and upgrading technology using categorical funds.

Delving deeper into the varied areas associated with instructional technology, one can find that there are five fundamental components that foster quality technology in a school district.

The first component has to do with having a written plan for technology. Many dollars can be wasted when a district technology plan does not exist. Many model templates for technology planning exist. Leading companies like IBM and Xerox now provide services to school districts for technology planning. To improve student achievement, it is highly recommended that a school district first organize a quality technology plan based on the realities of the district. The school district's technology plan

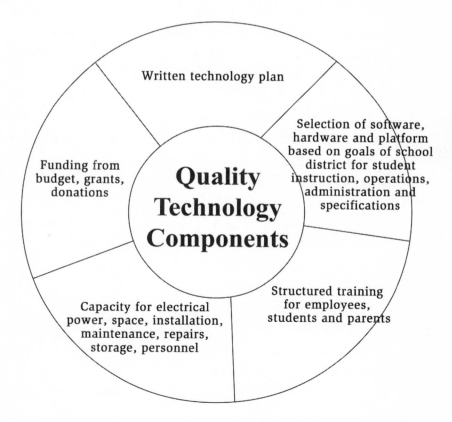

Written technology plan

Selection of software, hardware and platform based on goals of school district for student instruction, operations, administration and specifications

Funding from budget, grants, donations

Quality Technology Components

Capacity for electrical power, space, installation, maintenance, repairs, storage, personnel

Structured training for employees, students and parents

7

should focus on improving student achievement and fostering proper school administration. Without a plan, the desire of a district for a "racehorse" technology offering could come out looking like a camel. Planning is critical, essential, and fosters sensitivity to limited funds.

The second component has to do with hardware and software. What platform, brands, and software specifications will be considered for use in the district or school? In the early days of instructional computers and software, Apple products were considered most available and user friendly for K-12, especially elementary schools. With the passage of time, many school districts are going with a unitary platform, either all Apple/Macintosh, or all PC/IBM. At the high school level, some schools are committed to providing students opportunities to learn using both of the major platforms, Apple and IBM. In the minds of some people, the issue of the type of platform is no longer important, with new software and programs compatible with both platforms. Operationally, it is wise for school districts to establish clear guidelines and regulations related to selecting and purchasing hardware and software. Again, major attention should be placed on the fostering of high student achievement and administrative efficiency, not just fads and fancies of the time.

The third component has to do with training. Without proper training, technology can sometimes be of little value. It does not make sense to purchase hardware and software, then provide no training to employees. Such action is analogous to purchasing a car and never learning to drive. In the scheme of things related to technology, staff development/training is an imperative. There exist unfortunate stories of school districts ordering large numbers of computers and varied software packages and, years later, finding much of the things ordered still

7

unpacked in boxes because no one was ever trained to use the things purchased.

The fourth component has to do with capacity. Implementing technology today often requires additional electricity, space, air conditioning, furniture, staffing, and security. Many school districts are finding that when they turn on all of their computers, copiers, scanners, and lights, they blow out fuses and breaker boxes, and the lights go out. Such cases usually indicate insufficient electrical power to the building. It is wise and highly recommended that school districts periodically conduct an electrical needs assessment in order to plan for the future. Additionally, serious consideration should be given to the space required for technological hardware and software. Most schools built shortly after World War II were not designed to provide space and power for modern computers. It is highly recommended that school districts bring in architectural planners to provide recommendations for improving the use of space in order to properly use computers and other technologies in schools. Additionally, proper staff must be employed to install, service and maintain the computers, servers, routers and other technology equipment required in schools today.

7

The fifth component has to do with funding for technology. It is generally known that technology is now imperative in the instruction of students and the administration of schools. The issue of finding the dollars to pay for such technologies ultimately surfaces and must be addressed. The hard answer is simply that the adults, the parents and other taxpayers, have to decide that they are willing to provide funding for technology in the schools. The students do not have the wherewithal to fund technology. They can only buy so much by selling candy. And why should they have to sell candy or do other fundraisers to garner funds for such a vital part of their education? Good planning by adults is the key. Having a high quality, well-thought-out technology plan, properly communicated to adults in the community, could go a long way in garnering the support needed to fund technology. The reality of life today is that many people are leery of spending more of their earnings for schools. Actually, it is difficult getting voters to approve bonds and millages.

School districts that are economically challenged often face multiple challenges. In some areas, voters refuse to pass bonds to upgrade school buildings and technology. These areas often have declining tax bases. These areas often have home conditions that do not include computers. Yet all students are being asked to achieve at high levels in this age of technology, as mandated by good educators and NCLB. The answers for students in such areas are often complex, yet the answers do exist. Churches, public libraries and other service institutions are now beginning to provide computers and labs in economically challenged communities. Many school districts in such areas are using their entitlement funds from Title I, II, V, and VI to provide computers and other technologies in schools that qualify. Many local businesses and corporations are providing grants, donations, and partnerships to foster the upgrading of technology in schools.

The area of technology is vital to the improvement of student achievement. Today, students without access to technology will definitely be left behind. It is incumbent on the adults, not students, to make sure that all steps are put forth to provide proper technologies to students and school administration in order to foster high student achievement. Technology in education today is not an option; it is a requirement. Adults hold the key to student achievement in this area.

Provide Proper Technology for
Instructional and Administrative Uses

Footnotes

[1]Bill Gates, *Business @ the Speed of Thought*, (New York: Warner Books, 1999), 3.

[2]Ibid., xvii.

7

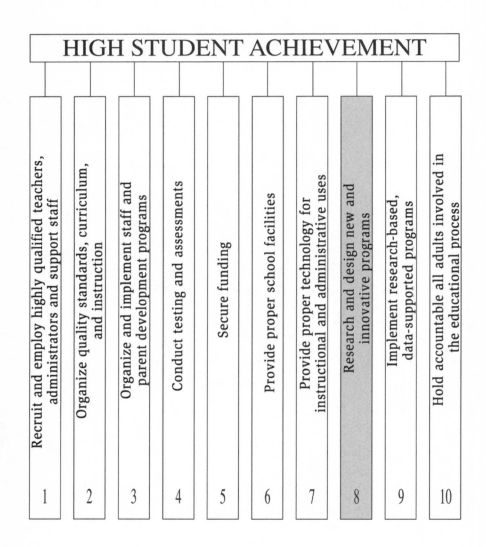

HIGH STUDENT ACHIEVEMENT

1. Recruit and employ highly qualified teachers, administrators and support staff
2. Organize quality standards, curriculum, and instruction
3. Organize and implement staff and parent development programs
4. Conduct testing and assessments
5. Secure funding
6. Provide proper school facilities
7. Provide proper technology for instructional and administrative uses
8. Research and design new and innovative programs
9. Implement research-based, data-supported programs
10. Hold accountable all adults involved in the educational process

Ten essential strategies for adults supporting high student achievement.

STRATEGY NUMBER EIGHT:

Research and Design
New and Innovative Programs

There is a wise old statement that goes like this: "If you continue doing things the way that you have always done them, the chances are great that you will continue getting the same results that you have gotten in the past." Of course, this statement can be interpreted in two or more ways. The positive interpretation is that doing things the same old way results in consistency, continuity, and results that are predictable. There are certain things in life that we like the way they are in their present forms. Certain products, foods, recipes, flowers, perfumes, clothing styles, shoes, mattresses, music, art, sports, architecture, and many others elements in our daily lives have become commonplace. We like them the way they are and desire no changes in our favorites. We often react negatively when our favorites are tampered with. For example, many people became upset with the Coca-Cola Corporation when changes were made briefly in the ingredients for the Coca-Cola soft drink. After a short period of time, and after reviewing the fallout from the changes, Coke reverted to the old formula in response to customer demands. People were happy with the product and did not want it to be changed.

On the negative side of the statement, the implication is that changes should be made when past actions, practices and pro-

8

grams are not producing the desired results. Why continue doing things that are not supporting the objectives for improvements? Some characterize the practice of the continued used of unproductive actions and unproductive practices as insanity. I liked the saying of my grandfather, who often admonished us with the following statement: "If your horse dies, dismount." In other words, plan to sunset or revise programs, practices, and actions that are not bearing results.

Another motivating statement applicable to the concepts of this chapter is the following: "God blesses the child that has his/her own." The implication of this statement is that working to have your own property, programs, and practices can often be a plus. The statement also can serve as a motivator to individuals and organizations to launch out into the deep by creating new and innovative programs, practices, and actions in order to produce improved results. If handled correctly, innovations can often catapult individuals and organizations into the future as opposed to remaining in the security of the present. Innovation, thus, can propel us into thinking in the future tense.

Care, common sense and ethics must always accompany innovations. Innovation void of research can sometimes result in catastrophic harm and failure. Innovation for innovation's sake can be invaluable in certain segments of our society — technology and corporate inventions, for example. In other segments, poorly designed innovations might be deadly and financially risky.

The elements of research and development (R & D) are common in corporate and scientific areas. In education, we are finally accelerating our imaginations and becoming more creative in developing programs to improve student achievement. Areas of education, especially public schools and higher education, have been forced by elements of competition to improve

8

Research and Design
New and Innovative Programs

or go out of business. The business principle of providing the best for the customer is evolving in the field of education, spurred by competition.

In the last two decades of the 1900s, foreign automobile makers began taking greater shares of American car buyers. In the 1950s and 1960s, products made in certain foreign countries were generally thought of as junk with little value. In the 1970s, as many foreign countries became innovative and modern, their products improved and their customer base grew with the improvements and innovations. In the United States, by 1980, driving a foreign car became a status symbol in many parts of the country.

The research element has been often overlooked. Research is often done behind the scenes. Many corporations, for business reasons, cloak their research elements in strict confidence in order to hinder other corporations from stealing their ideas. In order to remain competitive, many corporations have think tanks and creative invention centers organized solely to come up with new and innovative products and inventions. As a school principal and superintendent, I had the opportunity to visit and tour many corporate institutions that focused their entire work on researching and creating innovations. Batteries of engineers, scientists, artists, chemists, tool makers, and system designers were often hired and placed in work locations and charged with transforming ideas into real products.

The time has arrived for schools, especially public schools, to take the opportunity to design and implement innovative programs for improved student achievement. Many school districts are seizing the opportunity by being creative in implementing a series of new and innovative programs. Many school leaders now realize that some of the old/traditional programs and practices have outlived their usefulness and are in need of

8

being improved or replaced with new and innovative programs. Just as in business, the automobile industry, and other corporate areas, educational leaders, especially public school educators, are receptive to rolling out their "new and improved" educational programs in order to compete. With the growing popularity of charter schools, private schools, parochial schools, home schooling, online schooling, and other innovations in the area of education, the traditional public school model is being challenged to compete or go out of business. Parents today have a much wider array of school choices from which to select for their children. No longer do local public schools have the lock on the children that live in their school attendance zones. Parents today are exercising their rights to have their children attend the schools that are of high quality — usually meaning good test scores, good teachers, good curriculum, and a high degree of safety. In some areas, the issues of vouchers and charter schools have been at the heart of the actions propelling competition and innovation.

There is a large body of educational theories and research supporting innovations for schools. Because curriculum and schools are dynamic and subject to change, creative scholars, researchers and others will provide concepts for review. Following is a listing of key concepts and theories that have been influential in fostering the incubation of innovation in education:

National Education Goals, 1989

The concept for the establishment of national goals came out of the 1989 Education Summit in Charlottesville, Virginia. That summit also spurred the later enactment of the Goals 2000 Educate America Act of 1994. The National Education Goals selected were as follows:

Research and Design
New and Innovative Programs

Goal 1: Ready to Learn. By the year 2000, all children in America would start school ready to learn.

Goal 2: School Completion. By the year 2000, the high school graduation rate would increase to at least 90 percent.

Goal 3: Student Achievement and Citizenship. By the year 2000, all students would leave grades 4, 8, and 12 having demonstrated competency over challenging subject matter including English, mathematics, science, foreign languages, civics and government, economics, arts, history, and geography, and every school in America would ensure that all students learn to use their minds well, so they may be prepared for responsible citizenship, further learning, and productive employment in our nation's modern economy.

Goal 4: Teacher Education and Professional Development. By the year 2000, the nation's teaching force would have access to programs for the continued improvement of their professional skills and the opportunity to acquire the knowledge and skills needed to instruct and prepare all American students for the next century.

Goal 5: Mathematics and Science. By the year 2000, the United States would be first in the world in mathematics and science achievement.

Goal 6: Adult Literacy and Lifelong Learning. By the year 2000, every adult American would be literate and would possess the knowledge and skills necessary to compete in a global economy and exercise the rights and responsibilities of citizenship.

Goal 7: Safe, Disciplined, and Alcohol and Drug-Free Schools. By the year 2000, every school in the United States would be free of drugs, violence, and the unauthorized presence of firearms and alcohol and would offer a disciplined environment conducive to learning.

8

Goal 8: Parental Participation. By the year 2000, every school would promote partnerships that would increase parental involvement and participation in promoting the social, emotional, and academic growth of children.

Secretary's Commission on Achieving Necessary Skills (SCANS), 1992

This was a concept developed by distinguished representatives from education, business, labor and government. The group developed a final report entitled "Learning a Living: A Blueprint for High Performance: to encourage a high-performance economy characterized by high-skills, high-wage employment." The concept called for educators to incorporate the following competencies into curricula and instructions:

Workplace Competencies
Effective workers can productively use:
A. Resources: allocating time, money materials, space, staff;
B. Interpersonal Skills: working on teams, teaching others, serving customers, leading, negotiating, and working well with people from culturally diverse backgrounds;
C. Information: acquiring and evaluating data, organizing and maintaining files, interpreting and communicating, and using computers to process information;
D. Systems: understanding social, organizational, and technological systems,
E. Technology: selecting equipment and tools, applying technology to specific tasks, and maintaining and troubleshooting technologies.

8

The Foundation Skills

Competence requires:

A. Basic Skills: reading, writing, arithmetic and mathematics, speaking and listening;

B. Thinking Skills: thinking creatively, making decisions, solving problems, seeing things in the mind's eye, knowing how to learn, and reasoning;

C. Personal Qualities: individual responsibility, self-esteem, sociability, self-management and integrity.[1]

Learning Styles and Multiple Intelligence

A. Learning Styles
1. *Visual Learners,* learn through seeing
2. *Auditory Learners,* learn through listening
3. *Kinesthetic Learners,* learn through moving, doing and touching

B. Multiple Intelligence, seven ways to demonstrate intellectual ability as organized by Howard Gardner
1. *Visual/Spatial Intelligence.* The ability to perceive the visual. Students think in pictures and vivid mental images to retain information. Students like looking at pictures, movies, maps, charts, videos, and graphs.
2. *Verbal/Linguistic Intelligence.* The ability to use words and language. Students have highly developed auditory skills and speak well. Students think in words instead of in pictures. They learn from listening, speaking, writing, explaining, and story telling.
3. *Logical/Mathematical Intelligence.* The ability to use reason, logic and numbers. Students think conceptually in logical and numerical patterns. They learn from prob-

8

lem solving, and abstract concepts. Experimenting, complex mathematical calculations, geometric shapes.

4. *Bodily/Kinesthetic Intelligence.* The ability to control body movement and handle objects with skill. Students express themselves through movement. Students have good eye-hand coordination and a good sense of balance. They learn from acting, marching, dancing, sports, and movements.

5. *Music/Rhythmic Intelligence.* The ability to produce and appreciate music. Students inclined musically to do things in rhythms, sounds, melodies, and patterns.

6. *Interpersonal Intelligence.* The ability to communicate, relate and understand others. Students seek to understand how other people think and feel.

7. *Intrapersonal Intelligence.* The ability to reflect on self and be aware of one's inner state of being.[2]

Phonics in Reading Instruction

The teaching of phonemes, the smallest unit of sound used in communicating with others.

Literature Based/Whole Language Reading Instruction

In this model for the teaching of reading, students are provided materials at the level of their interest. Students progress to different levels of reading materials based on their interests.

Core Curriculum Learning

This is a curriculum model begun by Professor E. D. Hirsch, Jr. through the Core Knowledge Foundation. The

8

model is organized to have elementary students learn selected core knowledge organized in sequence for each grade.

Value-Added Instruction and Assessment

This concept was developed by Bill Sanders, a professor at the University of Tennessee. The model gauges student performance over time, based on a series of complex statistical scores and test results. The model is used to foster student achievement based on quantifiable data. The model also fosters accountability of teachers and administrators.

Volumes of research, concepts, reports and ideas exist supporting the notion of innovations to foster improvements in student achievement. From the Progressive period works of John Dewey to the present, educators have been watchful for innovative models to integrate into the curriculum of schools across the country. The research foundation for innovations is clear and replete with a wide spectrum of models and concepts. The challenge to school districts is to wade through the vast number of innovations with the objective of finding those that might be helpful to the students to be served.

It is common for school districts to develop their own innovative concepts and assessments. Improving schools from within is an approach that can be fulfilling and worthwhile for implementation and ownership. People tend to have stronger attachments to programs that they design themselves for their own students. The challenge for most schools, however, has to do with finding the time for creative development of programs. Also, the issue of funding eventually emerges. Most people do not want to spend their time developing new and innovative programs that cannot be funded or implemented. In past years,

8

most school districts have had limited funds to support the implementation of new programs.

As in the previous strategies, adults hold the power to make things happen for students. In most cases, adults in school districts are responsible for the organization of curriculum and funding, not students. If new and innovative programs are to take place in school districts, the adults will have to be marshaled to provide the needed support and funding. Adults hold the key to new and innovative things happening in a school district.

Footnotes

[1] Howard Gardner, *Frames of Mind: The Theory of Multiple Intelligences* (New York, Basic Books, 1993).

[2] *The Teacher Handbooks* (Charlottesville, VA: Core Knowledge Foundation).

8

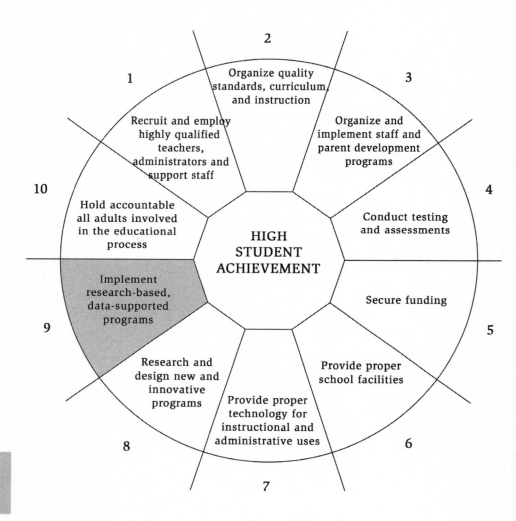

Ten essential strategies for adults
supporting high student achievement.

STRATEGY NUMBER NINE:

Implement Research-Based, Data-Supported Programs with Proven Success

Students in schools make up a captive audience that is largely at the mercy of a host of adults that provide leadership, teaching, and support for the schools. The adults, hopefully, are committed to always working to improve student learning by providing to students under their charge programs that work. There is an inherent trust from students that the adults will always do those things that are in the best interest of students. Students depend on adults to do the right things.

A key pillar supporting student achievement includes the process of selecting and implementing programs that are research-based and data-supported to improve student achievement. Adults are the key players in this process.

During my more than three decades of work in the field of education, I have seen hundreds of educational programs and pedagogical models on the market, all professing to ultimately improve student achievement. I have seen very high quality programs with substance. I have also seen programs that were of little substance being promoted by hucksters only interested in financial gain instead of student achievement. I have seen people with little or no training or experience in education mas-

9

querading as education experts, charging large speaking and presentation fees to the detriment of many people.

Because of the seriousness of the topic, special effort is being made by educators to focus greater attention on the process and the products involved in the selection and implementation of programs to improve student achievement. This strategy of basing the selection and implementation of programs on organized guidelines and common sense is gaining notoriety. With NCLB and many current grants, school districts are being encouraged strongly to make changes necessary to implement new, research-based, data-supported programs. The idea is taking root and is being taken seriously in a very large number of schools and school districts across the United States.

The idea is great. The process is, however, complex and fraught with challenges. The process of selecting and implementing programs can be seen as a positive opportunity to ultimately help student learning, or it can be seen as an unwelcome nightmare. It is my contention that, without ignoring the inherent complexities, the process of selecting and implementing new programs can be worthwhile and rewarding to students and all adults involved when the following seven basic steps that I have organized and used are followed:

Steps in the Selection Process

1. Conduct a needs assessment of the academic needs of students.
2. Research and study the various available programs that relate to the needs of the targeted cohort of students. Involve a cross-section of staff along with parents and students in the process.
3. Select two or three of the programs for on-site visitations.

4. Visit schools to see the programs in action and to talk directly with students, teachers, administrators, and parents involved in the program. Review data related to the programs at the local sites.
5. Organize funding sources and budget costs for programs.
6. Do your homework related to the programs under consideration.
7. Select the program that best fits the needs of your students.

The selection process, when followed properly, will increase the possibility of success. Because the adults are dealing with the education and lives of students, proper care and attention must be paid to making wise and meaningful decisions. The stakes are too high for major errors to take place. Keep in mind that if a horse is needed, one should not select an elephant.

Just as there are steps in the selection process, likewise, there are many steps involved in implementing new programs in schools or school districts. Selection is phase one. Implementation is phase two. Following are the five key steps in implementing new programs:

Steps in the Implementation of New Programs

1. Involve a cross section of the staff, parents, and students in the implementation phase.
2. Secure proper approvals for implementation.
3. Make sure that proper funds are appropriated for the program. It is best when programs are funded properly before implementation. It can be a real downer for the staff, administrators, students and teachers when programs are not implemented due to lack of funding. Not having proper funds for needed programs can be taxing to staff morale and

9

trust. It is discouraging for employee morale and trust when new programs that they participated in selecting are trumpeted for implementation, then quashed because of the lack of funds. Be leery of attempting to implement programs without the needed funds and supporters. Remember, programs that are included in the budget of your school board and building plans are deemed important.

4. Conduct the proper staff training required for the program. Avoid the "training in flight" approach. To improve the chance of success for any new program, the proper training is imperative.

5. Implement monitoring and evaluation of programs to make sure that they will meet the needs of the targeted students and produce expected outcomes.

Help from a variety of outside sources can be provided to school districts in selecting researched, data-supported programs. Providers of such assistance include the United States Department of Education in Washington, D.C.; state departments of education in the various states; regional education resource centers; and a host of others (including Phi Delta Kappa, various associations, and private consultants).

The catchphrase in the selection and implementation phases has to be "I hear what you are saying, but show me the research and the data." Selecting and implementing new programs to improve student achievement can be complex, time consuming, and worthwhile. All of the hard work required in the process can be celebrated when it results in improved student achievement. The ultimate goal is always the improvement of student achievement.

Having progressed from teacher to department head, assistant principal, principal, curriculum administrator, assistant

9

Implement Research-Based, Data-Supported
Programs with Proven Success

superintendent and, finally, superintendent, I have participated in, led, and observed the selection and implementation of a very large number of new programs. Most of the programs were research-based and data-supported. Some of the programs were implemented based on education fads or the new "flavor of the month," and on pure educational hunches. In most cases, the researched, data-supported programs produced better results in student achievement.

Educators today are advocating the implementation of researched, data-supported programs. While I strongly support that notion, I hasten to interject the idea that there is sometimes justification for adopting new and untried programs. This cautionary idea is based on the notion that someone has to step out, take risks, and develop new ideas in education. In other words, there has to be room for innovation and experimentation in order for research and data gathering to take place. The idea is similar in some ways to the job search process for young college graduates. The young people go out looking for jobs and are told that they have the college degrees, but no experience, no work track record. The job seekers often reply that they have not been given the opportunities to develop work track records. Thus, employers often have to decide whether to hire people with proven track records or those with unproven records.

When adequate funding is available, often experience tends to prevail over non- experience in getting jobs. There are cases, however, when inexperienced workers are hired over experienced people in order to bring in new ideas and to cut costs — experienced workers tend to require higher salaries. In education, school districts often hire first year teachers rather than veteran teachers for budgetary reasons and to gain new ideas from recently trained college graduates.

9

Navigating the complex process of selecting and implementing new programs is never clean. It tends to be messy, even under the best of conditions. Human nature tends to resist change. Many organizations tend to resist change. So leading change with the selection and implementation of new programs will have accompanying roadblocks and barriers. Having clear goals, objectives, and a plan of action will be most helpful in overcoming the likely obstacles that naturally come about in the change process.

My experience has shown that planning, communicating and persisting are the key actions in fostering the needed changes to improve student achievement. Reinventing the wheel is not always necessary in the selection of programs. There are thousands of programs now available. The challenge is finding the right program to fit the needs of the targeted students. Clearly, researched programs with strong data support are the programs of choice and most highly recommended for schools or school districts that are seriously interested in improving student achievement.

Based on my many years of training and work experiences as an educator, I share with you the following listing of successful programs, pedagogy, and concepts that have supporting research and data:

9 Programs, Pedagogy, Research and Concepts For Improving Student Achivement
(See Appendix 2 for descriptions)

- Accelerated Schools (K-12)
- America's Choice (K-12)
- ATLAS Communities (PreK-12)

Implement Research-Based, Data-Supported Programs with Proven Success

- Basic Schools Network (K-12)
- Carbo Reading Styles Program (K-12)
- CELL/ExLL (PreK-6)
- Coalition of Essential Schools (K-12)
- Community for Learning (K-12)
- Co-nect (K-12)
- Core Knowledge (K-12)
- Different Ways of Knowing (PreK-8)
- Direct Instruction Model (K-8)
- Early Intervention in Reading (K-6)
- Effective Schools (K-12)
- Exemplary Center for Reading Instruction (K-12)
- Expeditionary Learning Outward Bound (K-12)
- First Steps (PreK-8)
- First Things First (K-12)
- High Schools That Work (9-12)
- High/Scope Primary Grades Approach to Education (K-3)
- Integrated Thematic Instruction (K-12)
- International Baccalaureate
- Junior Great Books (K-12)
- Literacy Collaborative (K-12)
- MicroSociety (K-8)
- Middle College (10-12)*
- Middle Start (5-9)
- Modern Red SchoolHouse (K-12)
- National Writing Project (K-16)
- Onward to Excellence (K-12)
- Paideia
- QuESt (K-12)
- School Development Program (K-12)
- Success for All/Roots & Wings (PreK-8)

9

- Talent Development High School with Career Academies (9-12)
- Talent Development Middle School (4-9)
- Turning Points (6-8)
- Urban Learning Centers (PreK-12)

Research Documents on School Improvement and Improving Student Achievement

Roland Barth, *Improving Schools from Within: Teachers, Parents, and Principals can Make the Difference*, (San Francisco: Jossey-Bass Publishers, 1990).

Education Week, "Studies Find Benefits from 'America's Choice'" April 21, 2004.

Christine Finnan, *Accelerated Schools in Action: Lessons from the Field* (Thousand Oaks: Corwin Press, 1996).

T. Corcoran and M. Goertz, " Instructional capacity and high performance," (*Educational Researcher* Vol. 24, no. 9, 1995), p. 27-31.

Wendy Hopfenberg, Henry Levin et al., *The Accelerated Schools Resource Guide* (San Francisco: Jossey-Bass Inc., 1993).

E. D. Hirsch, Jr., *The Core Knowledge Curriculum.*

Lorraine Monroe, *Nothing's Impossible: Leadership Lessons from Inside and Outside the Classroom* (New York: Public Affairs, 1997).

P. Black and D. William, "Inside the black box: Raising standards through classroom assessment." *Phi Delta Kappan*, 80, no. 2139-148, 1998.

United States Department of Education, *Turning Around Low Performing Schools* (Washington, D.C.: United States Department of Education, 1998).

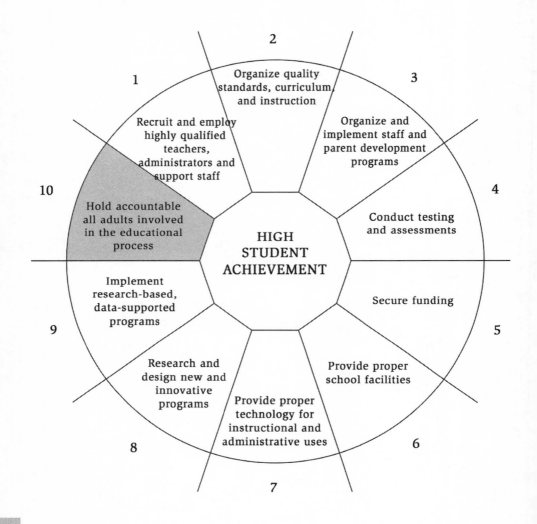

Ten essential strategies for adults
supporting high student achievement.

10

STRATEGY NUMBER TEN:

Hold Accountable All Adults Involved in the Educational Process

The watchword for the twenty-first century in education will be "accountability." The future of our democratic values and our nation will rest largely on the ability of our nation to educate all students to high standards in order for the United States to compete in the global society. Many details related to accountability will have to be researched, designed and implemented in order to further the causes that we hold dear in this country. Education is an institutional value that will remain in the forefront of our society for the century. As the melting pot of the world, the United States of the twenty-first century will remain committed to providing education to the "tired, the poor, the huddled masses yearning to breath free," as inscribed on the Statue of Liberty.

The Constitution of the United States delegates the responsibility of education to the states. States have taken up the mantle and established laws and codes for education. States have also delegated degrees of authority to local school boards of education for the education of the public school children in their regions. Some school boards have empowered individual schools with site-based management authority in order to foster greater ownership and motivation for student achievement.

10

125

Hundreds of organizational models have evolved, including the traditional centralized model and various forms of decentralized public school models. The beginning of the twenty-first century is witnessing an ever-growing number of chartered public schools, organized to provide a greater number of offerings and choices in education. Vouchers for use in the education of students are still being tested in the courts for possible greater use in the twenty-first century.

Even with all of the actions going on in education, the key question keeps returning: who will be ultimately accountable for the education of students? The answer to the question is very clear, yet complex. Contrary to the thinking of some people who believe that improving student achievement rests squarely on the shoulders of students, strong evidence now exists supporting the notion that adults are responsible for improving student achievement. Well, how do you like that concept?

It is very clear now to many people that for far too long the blame for low-achieving students has been placed on the students rather than on the host of adults who should be held accountable for having not fulfilled their responsibilities. The blame game for low student achievement in education has been around and used for many decades. Many college professors blame high school teachers for sending poorly educated students, many deemed unfit for higher level work, to their colleges. Many high school teachers blame middle grade teachers (middle/junior high) for sending them students unprepared for high school work. Many middle grade teachers complain that elementary teachers are failing to teach the fundamental grammar school skills to students, thus, the students are unprepared for middle grade work. Many elementary teachers complain that kindergarten, pre-kindergarten and nursery school teachers are being negligent in teaching children the early academic skills

10

needed for high quality elementary school work. Many elementary, kindergarten, pre-kindergarten and nursery school teachers blame the parents for sending them children with limited academic skills and limited home training. Many parents blame their doctors for having given them poor prenatal care and training. Many doctors blame their professors for having given them poor instruction in college — beginning the blame cycle again. The blame cycle often goes around and around and around with many people pointing at others as the cause for poor student achievement.

While humorous, the blame-cycle scenario truly exists in our society. When it comes to accountability for student learning, look out for finger pointing from adults. The finger pointing, when analyzed in detail, is only human. Few adults are big enough to take the blame for the failure of students, especially if there are obvious dysfunctions and weaknesses in educational design and delivery to students. People rarely step forward and take the blame for conditions that they cannot control. Thus, the accountability factor becomes complex. Again the question: who should be held accountable for the education of children?

Since schools and school districts are responsible for the delivery of curricula to students, some people believe that periodic audits of curricula might foster greater accountability and quality. Pioneered by Fenwick English, curriculum auditing calls for trained educators to "look under the rug" of curriculum to expose deficiencies in order to foster improvements.

Fenwick English organized the following five standards for use in the curriculum auditing process:

10

1. The school district is able to demonstrate its control of resources, programs and personnel.

2. The school district has established clear and valid objectives for students.
3. The school district has documentation explaining how its programs have been developed, implemented, and conducted.
4. The school district uses the results from the district designed or adopted assessments to adjust, improve, or terminate ineffective practices.
5. The school district has been able to improve productivity.[1]

As superintendent of the Buffalo School District, I recommended to the board of education that the district have a curriculum audit. The investment of nearly $50,000 in the audit produced valuable and objective observations, recommendations and lasting improvements related to the curriculum of the district. The curriculum audit fostered many changes needed to improve student achievement and greater accountability of adults charged with developing, teaching, and managing the curriculum in Buffalo.

There is an old adage that goes like this: "What gets measured, gets done." Paraphrased, the adage would state that "people get things done when they are held accountable for completing specific tasks." Leading change for accountability can be complex, rewarding, or a failure, depending on the skills of the person leading the change process. Leading change for accountability requires the establishment of a high sense of urgency and a low sense of complacency.[2]

Another statement from the past suggests that "the foundation of every state is the education of its youth." So, in some circles, the accountability factor for educating students rests on the state, not totally on the local schools. This concept serves as a key element in the philosophy inherent in the No Child Left

10

Hold Accountable All Adults Involved
in the Educational Process

Behind Act of 2001. The idea is that the states should establish standards and expectations for public schools and hold the schools responsible for meeting the expectations, period and without exception. The states must be the enforcers for accountability related to improving student achievement. Is that a form of accountability? Some would respond with a solid "yes." Others might respond with a host of responses to the contrary. Their ideas include the fact that states do not have the funding and staffing capacities to be the enforcers or the terminators for strict accountability. To highlight this point, the humorous idea is often presented about the state becoming like a dog chasing the tire on a moving car, then asking itself the following question: "What am I going to do with that car tire once I catch it?"

Of course, the states will play a leading role in the accountability sphere because NCLB is now law. As an education practitioner and as a researcher in education, I find clear evidence that NCLB is also forcing schools all across the country to be more accountable for improving student achievement. NCLB mandates are clear: standards, assessments, highly qualified teachers, annual progress toward objectives, feedback on student progress to parents and community, sanctions for low performing schools, and supplementary services to students. I also recognize that NCLB is not perfect: it suffers from inadequate funding, is limited in educational scope, calls for test-based accountability, and is utopian in tone. Love it or hate it, NCLB is definitely a force for greater accountability for adults. Student test scores ultimately reflect on the instructional and motivational strategies of adults.

The complexities inherent in the process of holding people accountable for improving student achievement can be ever expansive. The critical question keeps returning: Who are the people most accountable for improving student achievement?

10

Should students hold their teachers, school administrators, parents, government, community, business, and faith leaders accountable for their education? On the surface, the answer should be a resounding "yes" — all adults in a community are responsible for the education of students. That is the American design for education. Adults pool their dollars, usually in the form of taxes to pay for the education of their children in public schools. Some adults may elect to pay additional dollars above the taxes in the form of tuitions to private and parochial schools for a particular types of non-public education. Adults elect school board members to serve as their trustees for the schools. The school boards usually hire or elect superintendents to serve as the day-to-day chief operating officers for the school districts. The school board members make policies and the superintendents are responsible for implementing the policies. The superintendents serve as the quality controllers by recruiting and hiring qualified employees, organizing the curriculum, leading the delivery of the curriculum to the students, evaluating staff and student performances, developing staff development training, developing and managing the budget, taking care of school facilities, communicating with the public, working with the board of education, planning for the future, and a host other responsibilities. In general terms, the superintendent and the board of education are adults empowered and accountable for improving student achievement in school districts. In some circles, the superintendents are viewed as the head coaches, lead teachers, and administrators for the education of students. With proper board support, qualified staff, and proper funding, superintendents can lead educational activities that result in improved student achievement and they can be held accountable for the myriad of details involved in running school districts.

10

Hold Accountable All Adults Involved
in the Educational Process

The root concept of accountability is to hold someone or some group responsible for completing functions in education. The more specifically the functions are outlined, the easier the task of dealing with accountability. For example, those of us who fly as passengers understand the importance of expectations and accountability for pilots. We hold the pilots accountable for takeoffs, in-flight flying, and landing safely 100 percent of the time. We would refuse to be a passenger on a plane if a pilot came on the address system and proudly boasted of a record of only 70 or 80 percent safe takeoffs and landings. Our standard is safety 100 percent of the time while on planes.

As adults we must hold ourselves accountable for the education of all students, 100 percent of the time. Our goal is to have every student (100 percent) perform at the proficiency level for each grade level. Detractors of this notion suggest that such a goal is "pie in the sky rhetoric." Supporters of this concept suggest that the notion might be flawed in some areas, but it is a noble goal that can be reached. Just as airline pilots gladly accept the highest of expectations, teachers, principals, and parents must have the will to give every child a quality education. They must have the commitment to being accountable for getting every child across the finish line. Because there are no "throwaway students" anymore, the objective of all adults has to be to change from the "bell curve" mentality of the past to the "J-curve" theory for the future. As an underlying tenet of the No Child Left Behind Act, this change deserves additional explanation.

In brief, the bell curve concept in education states that achievement levels can usually be projected to fall into three categories, like segments of a bell (see below).

In segment one of the bell shape (the left segment) are the very low-performing individuals. In segment two are the aver-

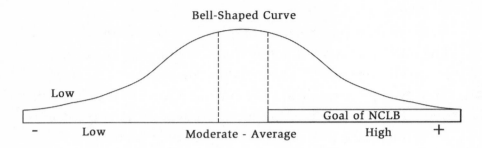

age-performing individuals. In segment three are the high-per-forming individuals. The theory suggests that this sorting will happen within almost every grouping of individuals. So, if you were sitting with two other individuals, this theory states that one of you will be low-performing, one will be average, and one will be high-performing. Where would you be placed on the bell curve?

Unfortunately, for centuries, the bell curve mentality has been the predominant concept in education. The SAT was implemented as a sorting instrument. Even today, various testing instruments are still being used to sort and "track" students in some K-12 schools. The bluebirds, the red birds, the robins, the cardinals, and the lowly sparrows — these "bird" mentalities still exist in the grouping of students, particularly in the elementary grades. New names are evolving to sort students such as ability grouping, magnet grouping and gifted grouping. Educationally and pedagogically, some students will require differentiated instruction. The key, however, is to move all students to mastery of the skills being taught — J-curve mentality. The bell curve mentality tends to foster the idea that there will always be a slow group.

The new theory that is moving into the educational field with lightening speed is the J-curve. This theory states that educational activities must be designed to move all students to the

10

level of proficiency in education. The theory rejects the notion that there has to be a low or failing group as suggested by the bell curve. The J-curve calls for all students to be winners and achievers at established, targeted levels.

J-Shaped Curve

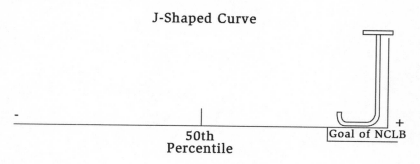

50th
Percentile

Goal of NCLB

The NCLB target is that all students will be proficient in targeted subjects by the year 2014. NCLB calls for states to establish progressional levels of achievement for students to reach annually until the 100 percent level is reached. The J-curve model is the realization of NCLB.

Footnotes

[1] Fenwick English, *Curriculum Auditing* (Lancaster: Technomic Publishing, 1988), 33-34.

[2] John Kotter, *Leading Change* (Boston: Harvard Business School Press, 1996), 4.

10

CONCLUDING THOUGHTS

The clarion call in education today is for improving student achievement. People from all walks of life are expressing interest in test scores, school rankings, and educational quality. There is an explosion of greater choices for educating students with the evolution of charter schools, vouchers, home schooling, and online schools. Public schools no longer have the lock on students in their attendance zones. Most people would truly like to have strategies that will result in all students achieving at their highest levels. This project presents ten strategies that, when properly implemented, will foster increased student achievement.

Historically, the institution of education in our society has transitioned from educating the elite few to educating all students. It has become important in our society to protect our democratic way of life by expanding educational opportunities to all students. It has become clear to our leaders through the years that the old adage has merit: "The foundation of every state is the education of its youth." The fundamentals of our republic have been brought to the forefront with the opening of doors for all to learn in the United States of America. Our country has moved through the agrarian and industrial periods and has entered the age of information and technology. It has progressed from horseback transportation to travel to the moon and back.

The movements which are opening the door to educating all students to high levels in this country have been led by many people, programs, and concepts. The founders of the early schools were resolute in providing opportunities for the teaching of reading, writing, and arithmetic. As Commander in Chief, President Abraham Lincoln was masterful in executing plans to conduct the Civil War and issuing the Emancipation Proclamation, thereby ending in this country one of the most brutal and inhumane institutions, slavery. John Dewey broke from traditional thinking and presented innovative and progressive concepts on teaching and learning. Thurgood Marshall was masterful in litigating the 1954 *Brown v. Board of Education* case that resulted in the legal ending of the separate but equal justification concept in American schools. President John F. Kennedy was bold in sending troops to open the doors to schools that had been shut to minority students. President Lyndon Johnson was creative in brokering a series of legislative actions that resulted in the war on poverty and the establishment of a wide array of social and educational programs. Dr. Martin Luther King, Jr., Rev. Jesse Jackson, Dr. Ralph Abernathy, and many others led marches to foster educational improvements and to end unjust treatment. Ron Edmonds was instrumental in presenting the concept that the adults in schools should take the responsibility for educating all students regardless of students' home life. Loraine Monroe has been proclaiming for decades that all students should be challenged with excellent leadership and high expectations in education.[1] President George W. Bush and Secretary of Education Rod Paige have been stalwart in their resolute standing for the No

Concluding Thoughts

Child Left Behind Act. Thousands of others have earned the right to be celebrated for their contributions to the goal of educating all students to high levels. Today, educating all children truly means all children, not just the elite.

Other projects and reports of note in the overall transformation of educational offerings in the United States include the 1985 report "A Nation at Risk," the book *Savage Inequality*, the SCANS Report that presented national goals for education, Goals 2000, and the Marshall Plan. Collectively, the work of people committed to the concept of improving student achievement in the melting pot of the world, the United States of America, has shown results.

The J-curve mentality has been elevated above the bell curve in education, as promulgated under No Child Left Behind. The J-curve fundamental point fosters the notion that standards and targets should be met by all students. The old bell curve presents the notion that, in groups, human beings perform at low, average or high levels. Thus, the bell curve supporters assumed that in schools there would always exist low- performing, average-performing, and high-performing students. Unfortunately, a plethora of data showed that the bell curve mentality in many schools was used to justify the acceptance of low-performing students, high minority placements in special education, tracking into low level courses, and traditional teaching pedagogy.

With the implementation of No Child Left Behind, education in the United Stated received a carrot and a stick. The "carrot" was in the form of a concept that all students would receive educational training based on state standards. The carrot called for annual testing to garner data about the progress of students toward targeted state and local goals. The "stick" in the process called for the restructuring of failing school with new programs, new teachers, new administrators, or charter school designation.

The stick called for the businesslike, hard-nosed approach of "produce continuous improvement or you're fired."

The carrot-and-stick elements now pervasive in education have driven teachers, administrators, parents, and even communities to coalesce in some areas. Teachers and administrators now realize that they must partner with parents and others in the community to educate students. The adage "educating everyone takes everyone" is becoming reality in many communities. No one wants to have his or her school labeled as failing. To avoid such a label, strategies are to be organized and implemented to ensure improvement in student achievement.

The African adage of "it takes a village to raise a child" is being revised in some circles to state that "it takes a village to educate a child." Improving student achievement in all schools in every section of the United States is ambitious and challenging. NCLB is committed to making the concept a reality. Adults are the people responsible for educating children. Adults with the will for high quality education can and will make improving student achievement the central theme of their existence in the community.

The ten strategies presented here are fundamental tenets related to adults for success in improving student achievement. Taken separately, each strategy is important. Students suffer when any one strategy is not properly implemented. Schools and school districts that are truly committed to improving student achievement are encouraged to fully implement all of the following strategies:

1.   Hire highly qualified people
2.   Organize and implement highly standards-based curricula
3.   Organize quality staff development and parent training
4.   Test and assess students at regular intervals to garner data

5. Work to secure proper funding
6. Provide students and staff with proper facilities
7. Provide proper technology for instruction and administration
8. Organize new and innovative programs
9. Select research-based programs
10. Hold all adults accountable in the education process

A wealth of data and programs exist about improving student achievement. This project adds to the knowledge base the critical concept that improving student achievement is proportionate to adults fulfilling their responsibilities and holding themselves accountable in the educational process. The concept of this project places the focus on adults, not students, for improving student achievement. Our students are depending on adults to fulfill their roles.

My best to all adults for increased commitment and fulfillment of the work assigned to us in providing high quality education to all students.

Footnote

[1]Loraine Monroe, *Nothing Impossible* (New York: Public Affairs, 1997), 174-193.

APPENDIX ONE:

1872 Rules for Teachers

(From the Oldest Wooden Schoolhouse, St. Augustine, Florida)

1. Teachers each day will fill lamps, clean chimneys.
2. Each teacher will bring a bucket of water and a scuttle of coal for the day's session.
3. Make your pens carefully. You may whittle nibs to the individual taste of the pupils.
4. Men teachers may take one evening each week for courting purposes, or two evenings a week if they go to church regularly.
5. After ten hours in school, the teachers may spend the remaining time reading the Bible or other good books.
6. Women teachers who marry or engage in unseemly conduct will be dismissed.
7. Every teacher should lay aside from each day's pay a goodly sum of his earnings for his benefit during his declining years, so that he will not become a burden on society.
8. Any teacher who smokes, uses liquor in any form, frequents pool or public halls, or gets shaved in a barber shop will give good reason to suspect his worth, intention, integrity and honesty.
9. The teacher who performs his labor faithfully and without fault for five years will be given an increase of twenty-five cents per week in his pay, providing the Board of Education approves.

APPENDIX TWO

Accelerated Schools. Founded by Henry Levin of Stanford University. A nationally acclaimed K-12 school improvement model characterized by collaborative programmatic planning by administrators, teachers, and parents for improvement in student achievement. Information on the model available from the National Center for the Accelerated School Project, University of Connecticut, 2131 Hillside Road, U-7 Storrs, Connecticut 06269. Telephone (860) 486-6330, Fax (860) 486-6348. Extensive research and information completed on the model. Two major publications on the model include: *The Accelerated Schools Resource Guide* by Wendy Hopfenberg, Henry Levin and Associates (a comprehensive guide presenting accelerated schools practices) and *Accelerated Schools in Action: Lessons from the Field* by Christine Finnan, et al.

America's Choice. Founded by the National Center on Education and the Economy (NCEE) in 1989. A nationally recognized K-12 school improvement model characterized by standards, assessments, aligned instruction, literacy and mathematics focus, and staff training. Unique features: looping in the elementary grades and interdisciplinary teaming in the secondary grades. As of 2004, this was the model being used in 547 schools serving approximately 350,000 students in 97 school districts in 16 states. Sample school sites: Dionne Warwick Institute in East Orange, NJ. Telephone (973) 266-5930; Intermediate School 93, grade 6-8, in Summerville, GA. Telephone (706) 857-3295. Information on model available from National Center on Education and the Economy, Suite 500 West, 555 12th Street, NW, Washington, D.C. 20004. Telephone (202) 783-3668, fax (202) 783-3672. Extensive research and information completed on the model. Model referenced in the following publications: "Inside the Black box: Raising Standards Through Classroom Assessment" by P. Black and D. William, printed in *Phi Delta Kappan* Vol. 80, No. 2, 1998; "Instruction Capacity and High Performance" by T. Corcoran and M. Goertz, printed in *Education Researcher* Vol. 24, No. 9: 27-31, 1995.

ATLAS Communities (Authentic Teaching, Learning, and Assessment for All Students). A PreK-12 curriculum model that focuses heavily on authentic, real-world activities for teaching and learning. The model calls for collaboration and articulation among the high school, middle school, and elementary school levels in selecting, teaching and assessing of skills to be taught. Students and teachers work together on topics that will result in solving real-world problems. Contact information: ATLAS Communities, Education Development Center, 55 Chapel Street, Newton, MA 02158. Phone: (800) 225-4276; Fax: (617) 969-3440; E-mail: aglas@edc.org; Web site: www.atlascommunities.org.

Audrey Cohen College: Purpose-Centered Education. A K-12 curriculum model that requires students to focus on a specific purpose every semester. The students take five Dimensions, or classes, that infuse many subjects and skills. The standards for the dimensions are fashioned at the Aubrey Cohen College.

Appendix

Schools participating in the model design instructional strategies to achieve a purpose each semester. Contact: Audrey Cohen College, New York City, NY.

Basic Schools Network. A curriculum model for elementary schools initiated by the Carnegie Foundation. The model focuses on the school as community, curriculum with coherence, climate for learning, and commitment to character. Contact: The Basic School Network, Virginia Tech NVC Rm. 459, 7054 Haycock Rd., Falls Church, VA 22043. Phone: (540) 568-7098. E-mail: parson@vt.edu

Carbo Reading Styles Program. A model for teaching reading in grades K-8. The model is designed to increase literacy by matching reading instruction to the student's preferred style of reading. The model calls for shared reading, choral reading, echo reading, and recorded books. Model being used in more than 1,000 schools. Teachers diagnose students' reading levels and implement strategies to improve their reading. Contact: National Reading Styles Institute, P.O. Box 737, Syosset, NY 11791. Phone: (800) 331-3117. Fax (516) 921-5591.

CELL/ExLL (Comprehensive Early Literacy Learning/Extended Literacy Learning). A comprehensive professional development program. The CELL portion of the training deals with the pedagogy of teaching literacy in grades K-3. The ExLL portion of the training focuses on teaching literacy in grades 4-8. The Second Chance at Literacy Learning provides support to secondary English instruction, grades 6-12. Contact: Foundation for Comprehensive Early Literacy Learning, 206 E. State Street, Redland, CA 92373. Phone: (909) 335-0826.

Coalition of Essential Schools (CES). A model for improving schools and student achievement organized in 1984

by Ted Sizer from Brown University. The model was originally designed for grades 9-12. It was later expanded to include grades K-12. The primary goal of the model is to help create schools where students can learn to use their minds. The model is characterized by (1) a set of common principles upon which schools base their practice, (2) personalized learning, (3) mastery of a few essential subjects and skills, (4) graduation by exhibition, and (5) a sense of community. Contact: Coalition of Essential Schools, Brown University, Box 1969, Providence RI 02912. Phone (401) 863-3384. Fax: (401) 863-2045. Web site: http://www.ces.brown.edu

Community for Learning (CFL). A school model designed to bring community resources into schools in order to foster student learning (churches, libraries, higher education institutions, community organizations, businesses, social service agencies, service organizations). Contact: Center for Research in Human Development and Education, Temple University, 1301 Cecil B. Moore Avenue, Philadelphia, PA 19122. Phone: (800) 892-5550. Fax: (215) 204-5130. E-mail: csmith6@vm.temple.edu Web: www.temple.edu/LSS

Co-nect. A consulting organization founded in 1992 by members of the Educational Technologies Group at Bolt and Newman, a research and development firm in Cambridge, Massachusetts. It specializes in working with schools and school districts in the areas of staff development, early literacy, effective use of technology, curriculum alignment, and use of data in decision making. Contact: Telephone (877) 726-6328 ext. 3186. Fax: (877) 726-7500. E-mail: info@co-nect.net

Core Knowledge. A curriculum organized under the leadership of professor emeritus at the University of Virginia, E.D. Hirsch, in 1986. The Core Knowledge Curriculum is organized to strengthen the learning activities for students in grades K-8.

Appendix

The curriculum prescribes four S's: solid, sequenced, specific, and shared. The curriculum provides a clear outline of content to be learned for each grade level. Contact: Core Knowledge Foundation, 801 East High Street, Charlottesville, VA 22902. Telephone: (434) 977-7550 or toll free (800) 238-3233. Fax: (434) 977-0021. E-mail: coreknow@coreknowledge.org

Different Ways of Knowing. An instructional model for K-12 schools. The model calls for intensive, multi-year professional development in the following six areas: 1) planning curriculum, instruction, and assessment using standards linked to big ideas; 2) facilitating teaching and learning that support student inquiry and self-directed learning; 3) teaching strategies that expert learners use in reading, writing, and mathematical thinking to close the achievement gap; 4) integrating the visual, performing, literary, and media arts in all content areas in service of learning for understanding; 5) engaging families and communities as partners in student learning; and 6) developing leadership for results inside a learning community. Contact: The Galef Institute, 11050 Santa Monica Blvd., Third Floor, Los Angeles, CA 90025. Telephone (310) 479-8883. Fax: (310) 473-9720. E-mail: sue@galef.org.

Direct Instruction Model. A model that requires the classroom teacher to provide direct instruction to students in groups or one-on-one settings. The model holds the teacher responsible for organizing and delivering instructional activities that will result in student learning. The model is based on the theory that children can learn at accelerated rates when teachers deliver instructions that are highly scripted and rapidly paced with immediate correcting of mistakes, students based in achievement grouping, and frequent student assessments. The following two organizations provide training and support in the model: National Institute for Direct Instruction, P.O. Box

1128, Eugene, OR 97440, Fax: (541) 683-7543; and the Association for Direct Instruction (800) 468-5850.

Early Intervention in Reading. An Internet-delivered professional development program for teachers of struggling young readers in grades K-6. The program focuses on the five essential elements of reading dealing with phonemic awareness, phonics, vocabulary development, reading fluency, and comprehension strategies. Contact: EIR Professional Development Program, 11293 Hastings Street NE, Blaine, MN 55449. Telephone: (763) 785-0701. Fax: (763) 785-0702.

Effective Schools. A concept and consulting organization championed by Dr. Lawrence Lezotte. Rooted in research on schools, the concept advocates the following correlates for schools to be effective: 1) safe and orderly environment; 2) climate of high expectations for success; 3) instructional leadership; 4) clear and focused mission; 5) opportunity to learn and student time on task; 6) frequent monitoring of student progress; 7) home-school relations. Contact: Lawrence Lezotte, Ph.D., Effective Schools, 2199 Jolly Road, Suite 160, Okemos, MI 48864. Telephone (800) 827-8041. Web: http://www.effectiveschools.com

Exemplary Center for Reading Instruction. A program that teaches elementary and secondary teachers (grades K-12) how and what to teach in reading and language arts instruction, and how to schedule classroom time. The program is organized to teach strategies that prevent student failure. The program teaches teachers the following strategies: 1) eliciting accurate and rapid response during instruction; 2) establishing high levels of mastery; 3) maintaining on-task behavior; 4) integrating the teaching of language skills; 5) using effective management and monitoring systems; 6) varying schedules and classes so students can invest the time and energy needed to learn; and 7) supervising students' hands-on activities and practice. Contact: Reid Foundation, 3310 South 2700 East, Salt Lake City, Utah 84109. Telephone: (801) 486-5083. Fax: (801) 485-0561. E-mail: ereid@xmission.com

Expeditionary Learning Outward Bound. A school improvement model that focuses on extensive content-based staff development. The model calls for students having educational experiences that involve learning expeditions that are long-term, in-depth studies of topics and themes that involve field work, service, adventure, and a cumulative final project or performance. The model was established in 1993 and grew out of Outward Bound, a non-profit organization established by Kurt Hahn in Britain in 1941 and brought to the United States in 1962. The main concept of the program involves key practices expeditions and field work. Contact: Expeditionary Learning Outward Bound, 122 Mount Auburn Street, Cambridge, MA 02138. Telephone: (617) 576-1260. Fax: (617) 576-1340. E-mail: meg_campbell@elob.org

First Steps. A professional development program organized to help K-5 teachers diagnose, teach, and monitor the progress of students in literacy development. The program consists of three components: 1) comprehensive materials, 2) professional development courses, and 3) school-wide implementation. The companion program for 6-12 teachers is Stepping Out. Contact: Steps Professional Development and Consulting, 97 Boston Street, Salem, MA 01970. Telephone: (866) 505-3001. E-mail: Julie_broz@stepspd.org

First Things First. A staff development and school organization model designed to focus on the following goals: 1) strengthening relationships among students and adults, 2) improving teaching and learning, and 3) reallocating budget, staff, and time to achieve goals 1 and 2. The model takes the following three complementary approaches to improving teaching and learning: 1) using schedules and staffing to give students more time in language arts and math and to lower student/adult ratios for as much of that time as possible; 2) working with all staff to increase the rigor of what they teach and to engage all students in learning; 3) identifying and supporting emerging instructional leaders to sustain a focus on teaching and learning. The model encourages the use of small learning communities. Contact: Institute for Research and Reform in Education, 1420 Locust Street, Suite 7Q, Philadelphia, PA 19102. Telephone: (215) 545-1335. Fax: (215) 545-3194. E-mail: laurielevin@irre,org

High Schools That Work. An initiative organized by the Southern Regional Education Board. Over 1,000 sites in 32 states are using the High Schools That Work program model. The HSTW program works to strengthen the academic preparation of vocational students by blending academic and vocational studies. Special emphasis is placed on having students reach performance goals in reading, mathematics, and science. Contact: Southern Regional Education Board, 592 10th Street N.W., Atlanta, GA 30318. Telephone: (404) 875-9211. E-mail: gene.bottoms@sreb.org

High/Scope Primary Grades Approach to Education. A curriculum for K-3 levels that provides guidelines for creating classroom learning environment, instructional materials, supplies, and equipment. Students work daily with a variety of manipulative materials, formulate practical problems, and make efforts to solve them. The curriculum calls for children to "learn by doing," and carrying out projects of their own choosing. Contact: High/Scope Educational Research Foundation, 600 North River Street, Ypsilanti, MI 48198. Telephone: (734) 485-2000. Fax: (734) 485-0704. E-mail: infor@highscope.org

Improving Schools from Within. A concept of school employees organizing themselves to solve school related issues. Concept presented by Roland Barth in his nationally acclaimed book *Improving Schools from Within.*

Integrated Thematic Instruction. A multi-level approach to teaching and creating a unique learning environment. The model calls for teachers to make learning vibrant by 1) anchoring curriculum to a year-long theme and rationale, 2) aligning district and state learning goals within a theme, 3) orchestrating "being there" experiences tied to meaningful content, and 4) reaching out to the community. The unique learning environment is characterized by 1) having the physical classroom to support the long-term learning, and 2) creating workable teams of students. ITI classrooms usually have soft lighting, neutral colors, live plants, curtains and lamps, and procedures for clarity of expectations. Contact: Integrated Thematic Instruction, Susan Kovalik & Associates, 17051 S.E. 272nd Street, Suite 17, Covington, Washington 98042. Telephone: (253) 631-4400. Fax: (253) 631-7500. E.mail: skovalik@oz.net

International Baccalaureate. Founded in 1968, the International Baccalaureate Organization works with over 1,426 schools in 117 countries serving approximately 200,000 students. The organization provides the following three programs: 1) the Diploma Program, 2) the Middle Years Program, and 3) the Primary Years Program. The IBO Diploma Program is a demanding pre-university course of study that leads to a series of examinations. The various IBO programs are designed for highly motivated students. Contact: IBO North America, 475 Riverside Drive, 16th Floor, New York, NY 10115. Telephone: (212) 696-4464. Fax: (212) 889-9242. E-mail: ibna@ibo.org

Junior Great Books. A professional development program organized to train teachers in inquiry-based instructional strategies, literary analysis, and critical thinking. The K-12 program is designed to stimulate interest among students in reading using interpretive activities. The program has been implemented in classrooms throughout the country. The program evolved from the Great Books movement launched in 1947 by Robert Maynard Hutchins, then president of the University of Chicago, and professor Mortimer Adler, a nationally recognized author. Contact: Great Books Foundation, 35 Wacker Drive, Chicago, IL 60601. Telephone: (312) 3325870. Fax: (312) 407-0224.

Literacy Collaborative. A long-term professional development program designed to provide comprehensive, school-wide approach to literacy instruction in the primary and intermediate grades. The program is designed for schools that have already made the commitment to a Reading Recovery program. The program requires teachers and administrators in the school and district to have entered into a collaborative long-term relationship with a regional university that is implementing a research-based Literacy Collaborative program. Contact: Literacy Collaborative Program, The Ohio State University, 807 Kinnear Road, Columbus, OH 43212. Telephone (800) 678-6486. Fax: (614) 688-3980.

League of Professional Schools. A program committed to helping schools become democratic institutions focused on student learning. The following three-dimensional framework are parts of the program: 1) Charter — the school's constitution that outlines the structure, conditions and procedures for democratic school-wide decision making that will bring the covenant to life; 2) Covenant — a guiding statement of a school's principles of learning, curriculum, instruction, assessment, professional development, scheduling, and allocation of resources; 3) Action research — a systemic way for schools to study the effects of educational programs on student learning. Contact: League of Professional Schools, 124 Aderhold Hall, University of Georgia, Athens, GA 30602. Telephone: (800) 578-2516. Fax: (706) 542-2502. E-mail: lewallen@uga.cc.uga.edu

MicroSociety. A K-8 program organized by Dr. George Richmond in the late 1960s. The program calls for students to create a microcosm of the real world inside of the school. Students have specific roles in running the activities of the microcosm. Contact: MicroSociety, 13 S. Third Street, Suite 500, Philadelphia, PA 19106. Telephone: (215) 922-4006. Fax: (215) 922-3303. E-mail: info@microsociety.org

Middle College. An alternative organizational model for providing education to high school students. The model calls for students to complete high school and college level courses concurrently. The model usually requires a partnership with a local community college for the college courses. Most models result in high school students graduating with a high school diploma and a college associate degree or certificate. Most middle college organizational models are customized by local school districts, chartering groups and partnering community colleges. Example of one middle college model: Washtenaw Technical Middle College High School in Ann Arbor, Michigan: (734) 973-3410.

Middle Start. A comprehensive program for schools with middle grades. The program calls for participating schools to develop the following: 1) Reflective review and self-study; 2) Effective small learning communities; 3) Rigorous curriculum, instruction, and student assessment; 4) Distributed leadership and sustainable partnerships. Contact: Middle Start Academy for Educational Development, 100 Fifth Avenue, New York City, New York 10011. Telephone: (212) 243-1110.

Modern Red SchoolHouse. A professional development program designed to help schools build coherent curricula that are aligned with state and local standards, improve teacher capacity to choose and implement effective instructional practices, and create college environments where the focus is on serving the needs of students. Contact: Modern Red Schoolhouse Institute, 1901 21st Avenue, South, Nashville, TN 37212. Telephone: (888) 275-6774, ext. 17. Fax: (615) 320-5366.

Monroe Doctrine. A leadership and pedagogical model organized by Professor Lorraine Monroe and presented in her nationally acclaimed book *Nothing's Impossible.* The concepts call for high expectations for teachers and students in order to garner high achievement.

National Writing Project. A nationwide professional development program for teachers. The program was organized in 1974 at the University of California, Berkeley, to improve the writing of students. The program operates in 46 states and Puerto Rico. The basic training is a five-week summer intensive institute for teacher leaders. The training focuses on examining how teachers teach writing; strategies for using writing as a tool for learning in all content areas; understanding the writing process by becoming writers themselves; studying the theoretical foundation of writing instruction and the research related to teaching writing; and preparing to become staff developers of their colleagues. Teachers trained during the summer return to their local schools and train other teachers. Contact: National Writing Project, University of California, 2105 Bancroft Way #1042, Berkeley, CA 94720. Telephone: (510) 642-0963. Fax: (510) 642-4545. E-mail: nwp@writingproject.org

Onward to Excellence. A school improvement model developed by the Northwest Regional Educational Laboratory in 1981

to help schools build capacity through shared leadership for continuous improvement. The model has the following seven school improvement outcomes: 1) Ensure quality and equity in the learning of all students; 2) Reach agreement about and secure widespread commitment to a mission and to student learning goals; 3) Ensure that what students learn, how they learn, and how they are assessed align with one another and with the mission and goals; 4) Ensure that the mission and goals drive human, financial, and other resource decisions; 5) Involve stakeholders who represent the community's diverse perspectives and cultural composition whenever planning and making improvements; 6) Collect and study data to improve decision making; 7) Create and sustain a learning organization that uses its own experience and knowledge, and that of others, in carrying out its work. Contact: Northwest Regional Educational Laboratory, School Improvement Program, 101 SW Main Street, Suite 500, Portland, Oregon 97204. Telephone (503) 275-9615. Fax: (503) 275-9621. E-mail: blumb@nwrel.org Website: http://www.nwrel.org/scpd/ote/

Paideia School. A school located in Atlanta, GA, founded in 1971 by parents who wanted an individualized, creative, and intellectually challenging education for their children. With more than 875 students from age three through twelfth grade, the school is fully accredited by the Southern Association of Colleges and Schools. In the school teachers frequently employ nontraditional means. At the elementary level, most academic work is done through individually prescribed instruction. Study is organized on a non-graded model. Students are encouraged to learn skills at a pace appropriate to their maturation levels regardless of standardized norms of grade levels. The emphasis is on individual achievement and challenge. Students learn the basic skills and content areas. They also learn skills in art, music, and physical education. Paideia is often considered as a community for families. Records from the school showed the Class of 2000 with 92 graduates, 16 National Merit Finalists, 5 National Achievement Finalists, 16 National Merit Commended students, and three National Achievement Commended students. The principles for the school are as follows: 1) excellence and hard work; 2) attitudes toward learning; 3) respect for diversity; 4) social responsibility; 5) egalitarianism; 6) empathy; 7) development of an ethical self; 8) commitment to an environmental view; 9) an appreciation of the importance of the present. Contact: The Paideia School, 1509 Ponce de Leon Avenue, Atlanta, GA 30307. Telephone (404) 377-3491.

Reading Recovery. A structured program to help low-achieving first graders (6-year olds) learn to read. Students selected for the program receive 30 minutes of daily one-on-one instruction for a period of up to 20 weeks. Elements of the program include the following: 1) teachers focus on each student's strengths; 2) students learn strategies that help them become independent readers; 3) students learn to read by composing and writing messages; 4) teachers base instruction on analysis of student knowledge and behavior; 5) students are taught to predict, confirm, and understand reading passages; 6) reading materials selected from over 2,000 small books of increasing difficulty. Contact: The Ohio State University Reading Recovery Program, 200 Ramseyer Hall, 29 West Woodruff Avenue, Columbus, OH 43210. Telephone (614) 292-7807.

School Development Program. This program was founded in 1968 by Dr. James Comer, a child psychiatrist at Yale University and Maurice Falk. The Comer Process is a school and system-wide intervention based on the theory that students learn better when they form strong relationships with the adults in their lives — teachers, parents, coaches, administrators, members of churches, community group leaders The process strives to relate child psychiatry and education. The process advocates that schools use the following six developmental pathways as framework in making decisions to benefit students: physical, cognitive, psychological, language, social, and ethical. Program is an approach for K-12 schools serving disadvantaged students. Contact: School Development Program, 53 College Street, New Haven, CT 06510. Telephone: (203) 737-1020. Fax (203) 737-1023. E-main: corvinjn@maspo3.mas.yale.edu Web site: http://www.info.med.yale.edu/comer

Success For All. A comprehensive restructuring program for elementary schools organized in 1987 at John Hopkins University. The program focuses on the following: 1) Emphasis on prevention, early and intensive intervention, and tutoring for students with academic difficulties; 2) Incorporation of state-of-the-art curriculum and instructional methods; 3) Emphasis on the integration of phonics and meaning-focused instruction, cooperative learning, and curriculum-based assessments; 4) Writing/language arts instruction emphasizing writer's workshops; 5) Pre-school/kindergarten instruction with storytelling and language development; 6) Adaptations for Spanish and English as a second language; 7) Family support program engaging parents, community members, and integrated services; 8) Extensive professional development throughout the elementary grades. Contact: Success for All, 200 West Towsontown Blvd, Baltimore, MD 21204. Telephone (800) 548-4998. Fax: (410) 324-4444. E-mail: sfainfo@success-forall.net

Talent Development High School and Middle School. A comprehensive school improvement model for large high schools seeking to improve attendance, discipline, achievement scores, and dropout rates. The model includes organizational and management changes to foster positive school climate, curriculum and instruction to prepare students for high-level courses in math and English, parent training, and professional development for employees. Contact: Center for Social Organization of Schools, John Hopkins University, 3003 N. Charles Street Suite 200, Baltimore, Maryland 21218. Telephone: (410) 516-8800. Fax: (410) 616-8890. E-mail: web-master@csos.jhu.edu

The Foxfire Approach. An approach to teaching and learning characterized by the creation of classrooms with strong community connections where learning grows out of student interest, high standards, and high expectations. The approach is further characterized by student involvement and action, thoughtful reflection and rigorous assessment, imagination and problem solving, applications beyond the classroom for learning, and meaningful connections to the community. The approach calls for students to build the ability to work collaboratively and assume responsibility for their own learning.

Contact: Foxfire Fund, Post Office Box 541, Mountain City, GA 30562. Telephone: (706) 746-5828. Fax: (706) 746-5829. E-mail: foxfire@foxfire.org.

Turning Around Low Performing Schools. "Turning Around Low Performing Schools" is a compilation of strategies and suggestions that have been instrumental in improving schools and student achievement in a number of cities. Report published by the United States Department of Education, Washington, D.C.

Turning Points. An organization model for schools servicing students in grades 5-9. The model calls for teachers to be coached in tested, effective instructional methods developed specifically for the middle-level learner. Contact: Center for Collaborative Education, 1135 Tremont Street, Suite 490,

Boston, MA 02120. Telephone (617) 421-0134. Fax: (617) 421-9016. E-mail: turningptsinfo@ccebos.org

Urban Learning Centers. A concept for providing an academically rigorous curriculum that connects across grade levels supported by parents and community. The concept includes the three key elements of 1) teaching and learning, 2) governance and management, and 3) learning supports. The model from the concept is a collaboration of the Los Angeles Unified School District, United Teachers of Los Angeles, and the Los Angeles Educational Partnership. Contact: Urban Learning Centers, 315 West 9th Street, Suite 1110, Los Angeles, CA 90015. Telephone: (213) 622-5237. Fax: (213) 629-5288. Web site: http://www.lalc.K12.ca.us

GLOSSARY

Ability Grouping. Assigning students of like skills to academically performing groups in order to provide instructional activities at their level. This instructional process is liked by many teachers because it allows for students at similar levels to work and learn together. There are other teachers who view ability grouping as another form of tracking students — the syndrome of the red birds, bluebirds, and sparrows.

Accountability. A process for holding an individual, a group, or an organization responsible for performing assigned tasks and functions.

Administrative Technology. Tools, equipment, and systems used by administrators in the execution of their leadership functions inclusive of computers; electronic data storage, management, retrieval, and manipulation; electronic payroll systems; electronic student information systems; communications/e-mail.

Affective Curriculum. Curriculum activities focused on teaching skills related to feelings, behavior, and character.

Assessment. Review of multiple elements relating to an individual, groups, or institutions. Often used synonymously with "testing." Tends to be broader in scope than testing.

Association of School Curriculum Directors (ASCD). A national organization that specializes in curriculum training and research.

Bell Curve. A concept in psychology and education that suggests that the distribution of human group performances will usually result in low, middle, and high levels. The concept suggests that the majority of people in groups perform at the middle/average level — like the hump in a bell. This concept is often challenged because it purports that low performers will exist in every group.

Bilingual Education. A program organized to teach English to students whose primary languages are other than English.

Board of Education. The governing body of a school district.

Brown v. Board of Education. A landmark case that resulted in the 1954 court ruling that the separate but equal practice in schools was unconstitutional. The ruling provided the legal justification for the movement to integrate schools.

Business Model. A concept that schools should be held accountable for targeted student results just like businesses target profits. The concept calls for parents to have choices in the selection of schools just like they have in the selection of goods in the business sector. The concept calls for unproductive schools to be closed — to go out of business — just like unprofitable businesses. Some educators refute the concept because they view schools and education as a social service organized to help students who often learn at different rates.

Charter Schools. Schools organized to be innovative and free from many of the standard regulations governing most public schools. Schools usually organized to provide additional and greater choices to parents in the selection of schools for their children.

Glossary

Civil Rights Movement. A period in American history characterized by African Americans and others striving to gain equal rights as provided under the Constitution of the United States. The period included such actions as Rosa Parks' refusal to give up her seat on a public bus; freedom marches; lunch counter sit-ins; school integration actions; voter rights initiatives; initiation of African American courses in schools and colleges; riots; The March on Washington; and leadership by Dr. Martin Luther King, Jr, Dr. Ralph Abernathy, Rev. Jesse Jackson, Rev. Benjamin Hooks, Thurgood Marshall, Roy Wilkins, Stokely Carmichael, Malcolm X, and thousands of other participants who supported the movement. Relating to schools, the movement resulted in the gradual integration of public schools in the country, particularly in the southern states. Longitudinal observations have shown that schools in the northern large cities became mostly segregated over time as the schools in the South became largely integrated, especially by the year 2000.

Cognitive Curriculum. A curriculum that is focused on student academic learning.

Common Schools Movement. A movement during the early days of the United States characterized by efforts to provide free education to children. Thomas Jefferson was instrumental in fostering the idea of providing education to the masses of white students.

Competitive Grants. Grants that are awarded based on competitive guidelines.

Cooperative Discipline. A process where teachers work together in planning structured strategies to improve the behavior of students with discipline problems.

Cooperative Learning. A process that calls for students to work in groups and teams. Individual members of the learning groups have assigned functions and responsibilities based on their interests and abilities.

Cooperative Teaching. Two or more teachers working together in structured planning and instruction of students. Synonymous with team teaching.

Council of Great Cities Schools. An association with membership consisting of the one hundred-plus largest school districts in the United States. The organization provides a variety of services to the districts related to organization, research, curriculum, and advocacy. Contact: Council of Great Cities Schools, 1301 Pennsylvania Avenue, N.W., Suite 702, Washington, D.C. 20004. Phone: (202) 393-2427. Fax: (202) 393-2400.

Core Curriculum. The fundamental body of knowledge and skills that some people believe all students should learn.

Curriculum. The sum total of everything taught and organized for students in a school or school district, written and unwritten.

Curriculum Alignment. A process of connecting teaching, curriculum, and testing to foster congruency, organization, and the improvement of student learning.

Curriculum Mapping. A formal and structured process of organizing selected skills for student learning over a period of time.

Curriculum Scope. A formal outlining of learning activities and concepts for student learning.

Curriculum Sequencing. A structured outline of the ordering of courses and learning activities. The order of the courses and activities usually follows the pattern of beginning level, intermediate level, advanced level. The concept follows the notion that learning takes place in incremental and sequential order.

Glossary

Dewey, John. An American educational philosopher and theorist who became known as the champion of the progressivism movement. Dewey worked at the University of Chicago and the University of Michigan. His educational concepts called for schools to be organized around the interests and experiences of children. He believed that students should be given projects to research and gain knowledge.

Differentiation. A process of teaching students who are at different academic levels. The process calls for the teacher to have a variety of learning activities that will provide opportunities for learning by the various levels of students in the class. The process calls for the teacher to organize rubrics that clearly indicate performance standards and work qualities.

Data Disaggregation. A process of dividing data into small segments for the purpose of analysis.

Developmental Assets/40 for elementary-age children. A listing of 40 developmental assets for elementary-age children compiled by the Search Institute of Minnesota.

Digital Nervous System. A concept coined by Bill Gates suggesting that organizations of the future will need to be connected via technology in order to be successful.

Direct Instruction. A method that requires the teacher to teach students directly.

Distance Learning. A plan that provides for student learning to take place at multiple locations using electronic means. For example, one teacher might teach a course to students located at multiple school sites. The distance learning rooms allow for visual and audio communications at all times among the individuals at the various sites.

Emancipation Proclamation. A proclamation made by President Abraham Lincoln ending the institution of slavery in the United States. The proclamation declared the ending of nearly four hundred years of inhumane treatment and slave status of African Americans in the United States.

Entitlement Grants. Grants allocated to schools based on the socio-economic and academic level of their students. The concept of the grants is that certain schools are entitled to the special funds because they serve students that require interventions that are costly.

Goals 2000. A set of goals for education that the nation hoped to reach by the year 2000.

Highly Qualified Teachers. A NCLB requirement that teachers be properly credentialed in the subjects that they are assigned to teach.

Home Schooling. Students are taught at home full-time instead of taking their classes in school buildings. Most parents serve as the teachers of their children involved in home schooling. Most states require students involved in home schooling to follow an organized curriculum.

Inclusion. The process of placing students with disabilities in regular classrooms with other students.

Industrial Revolution. The period of time in the United States, approximately 1900 to 1975, when the country moved from a total agrarian focus to a greater infusion of manufacturing production, especially in large cities. That period witnessed the invention, manufacturing and production of things that improved the standard of living, such as the automobile, food processing, clothing production, refrigeration and thousands of others.

Instructional Technology. Electronic tools, equipment, software, computers, and techniques for use in the classroom by teachers and students to foster learning.

High Priority Schools. A designation in the State of Michigan for schools that did not meet certain requirements under the No Child Left Behind Act.

Glossary

J-Curve. A concept that suggests that all students should show mastery of a set of learning concepts and skills. The concept does not allow for any student to fall into the low-performing category. Proficiency for all is the objective. This concept serves as the foundational core of the No Child Left Behind Act. NCLB calls for 100 percent of the students in schools to perform at the proficiency level on their state tests by 2014.

Looping. A system where a teacher keeps the same students for multiple years. For example, a teacher in a looping plan would teach the same students for first and second grades. The looping model is most frequently used in the elementary grades.

Mason-Dixon Line. The boundary line between Pennsylvania and Maryland surveyed by Charles Mason and Jeremiah Dixon during the years 1763 to 1767. Before the ending of slavery in the United States, the Mason-Dixon Line served as the line of demarcation between the free and the slave states.

Marshall Plan. A plan to improve large urban schools in the United States developed by the Council of Great City Schools, Washington, D.C.

Marshall, Thurgood. An attorney who won the landmark case, *Brown v. the Board of Education.* He was a major figure in the early days of the civil rights movement. He went on to become a Justice on the Supreme Court of the United States.

Michigan Education Assessment Program (MEAP). The annual statewide education assessment instrument used in the State of Michigan.

Nation At Risk Report. A report that was developed by a special commission organized by Secretary of Education Bell in 1983. The report made many claims about the American schools failing students.

National Conference of Governors. A group of governors that met annually to discuss strategies to improve education in their states and the nation. The council produced a set of recommendations embodied in the SCANS Report.

No Child Left Behind Act. A law passed in 2001 designed to improve schools in the United States. The law mandated that states set standards for the education of students and require schools to meet targeted annual yearly performance levels.

Pacing Instruction. An instructional model that calls for teachers to follow a timeline in the delivery of curriculum content. With the advent of high-stakes testing, many school districts have mandated that all teachers follow organized pacing charts to ensure that all students are given the opportunities to learn course content. For educational and legal reasons during this time of high stakes testing and exit examinations for courses and graduation, schools have organized the pacing of instruction to document dates and times for instruction.

Parks, Rosa. An early civil rights activist who, on December 1, 1955, refused to give up her seat in the "white" section on a public transportation bus to a white male in Montgomery, Alabama. For her action, Dr. Martin Luther King, Jr. referred to her as "the great fuse that led to the modern stride toward freedom." Her action was aligned with the concept of equality in education rendered in the *Brown v. Board of Education* results.

Pedagogy. The instructional strategy used by a teacher in the classroom to teach students.

Phonics. A system of teaching students to sound out word syllables. The system is used in many classes to teach word recognition and reading.

Progressivism. A theory and period in education characterized by a break from traditional instructional strategies. John

Dewey was recognized as one of the leading figures championing the tenets of progressive thinking in education.

Property Taxes. Taxes paid by owners of land and other properties. Schools in most states are funded primarily by property taxes.

Proration. A system where funds allocated to school systems are taken back from the school systems during the course of the fiscal year. This system is used in many states when the states anticipate running out of education funds before the end of the fiscal year. School districts dislike the proration concept because it tends to cause major budget problems for the districts. Prorations tend to cause major problems for school districts with limited rainy day funds.

Psychometrics. The field of mental measurement.

Reading Across the Curriculum. A concept that calls for all classes in schools to include reading activities.

Secretary's Commission on Achieving Necessary Skills (SCANS). A commission appointed by the Secretary of Labor to determine the skills young people need to succeed in the world of work. In 1992 the commission issued a report entitled "Learning A Living: A Blueprint for High Performance. A SCANS Report for America 2000."

Special Education. A federally mandated program to provide educational services to students with disabilities.

Sputnik. A spacecraft launched by the Russians.

Standards. A group of general statements in education expressing expected levels and qualities of instructional contents, pedagogies, and achievements. The No Child Left Behind Law of 2001 mandated that all states establish standards for learning in education.

Supplemental Services. A fancy name for tutoring and extra help. The No Child Left Behind Act mandates that supplemental services be provided to targeted students in schools that are in need of improvement. School districts fund supplemental services from their entitlement grant, Title I.

Team Teaching. A system where two or more teachers work with the same class of students. When working properly, team teaching allows for students to have more instructional attention from teachers.

Testing. An action or activity to examine the capabilities, knowledge and performance of an individual, class or organization on a set of pre-determined items.

Theme Schools. A concept that calls for schools to be organized around a central theme. The theme schools teach all of the fundamentals of a core curriculum with focused emphasis and extra attention to the theme area of the schools.

The Three Rs. Reading, writing and arithmetic.

Tracking. Placing students with like abilities in the same group for efficiency of instruction.

Unfunded Mandate. A requirement placed on a school or school district without the accompanying dollars needed to meet the requirement. Some school administrators view the federal requirements for No Child Left Behind and Special Education as prime examples of mandates that are not properly funded.

Value-Added Instruction and Learning. The sum of all teaching and learning during a period of time.

Vouchers. Public dollars given to parents to pay for the instruction of their children in private or parochial schools. The use of vouchers is still being contested in the courts. Some view the issuance of vouchers as a violation of the separation of church and state concept. Others view vouchers as dollars being used to prop up parochial schools and undermine the fiscal health of public schools. Still others view vouchers as a means

Glossary

for greater choice in educating students, especially those students who come from families with very limited financial means.

Whole Language. A method of teaching reading that calls for students to develop their reading skills by reading books and other materials of their interest. The method calls for a print-rich environment with a variety of printed materials at different levels. The method calls for students to learn to read by reading without major instruction in phonics.

Writing Across the Curriculum. A concept that calls for writing to be emphasized in meaningful ways in all classes.

Year-round Schools. An organizational design that calls for students to attend school at different periods during the entire school year, with shorter vacation breaks between sessions. This model is a necessity in some school districts with very large enrollments. Year-round schools are common in such cities as Los Angeles and Inglewood, California. Students still attend school between 175 and 190 days a year. The year-round feature includes the staggered scheduling of vacation times for students during the year. The educational values of year-round school are still being studied.

SOURCES CONSULTED

Books

Barth, Roland. *Improving Schools from Within: Teachers, Parents, and Principals Can Make the Difference.* San Francisco: Jossey-Bass Publishing, 1990.

Bellon, Jerry, Elner Bellon and Mary Ann Blank. *What Really Works: Research Based Instruction.* Knoxville, TN: Bellon & Associates, 1986.

Bennis, Warren. *Why Leaders Can't Lead.* San Francisco: Jossey-Bass Publishers, 1989.

Berliner, David and Bruce Biddle. *The Manufactured Crisis: Myths, Fraud, and the Attack on America's Public Schools.* New York: Addison-Wesley Publishing Company, 1995.

Bradley, Leo. *Curriculum Leadership and Development Handbook.* Englewood Cliffs: Prentice-Hall, 1985.

Broderick, Maria, Daniel Chazan, Sandra Lawrence, Paul Naso, and Bobby Starnes, Editors. *For Teachers About Teaching.* Cambridge, MA: Harvard Education Review, 1991.

Cawelti, Gordon, Editor. *Handbook of Research On Improving Student Achievement.* Arlington: Educational Research Service, 1995.

Church, Robert. *Education In the United States.* New York: The Free Press, 1976.

Covey, Stephen. *The 7 Habits of Highly Effective People.* New York: Simon & Schuster, 1989.

DuFour, Richard and Robert Eaker. *Professional Learning Communities At Work: Best Practices for Enhancing Student Achievement.* Bloomington: National Educational Services, 1998.

English, Fenwick. *Curriculum Auditing.* Lancaster: Technomic Publishing, 1988.

English, Fenwick. *Deciding What to Teach and Test.* Thousand Oaks: Crown Press, 2000.

Finnan, Christine, et al. *Accelerated Schools in Action: Lessons from the Field.* Thousand Oaks: Corwin Press, 1996.

Gates, Bill. *Business @ the Speed of Thought.* New York: Warner Books, 1999.

Gerstner, Louis V., Jr. *Reinvention Education: Entrepreneurship in America's Public Schools.* New York: Penguin Books, 1994.

Goodlad, John. *Teachers for our Nation's Schools.* San Francisco: Jossey-Bass Publisher, 1990.

Hill, Howard. *Effective Strategies for Teaching Minority Students.* Bloomington: National Educational Service, 1989.

Hirsch, E.D. *The Core Knowledge Curriculum.*

Hopfenberg, Wendy, Henry Levin and Associates. *The Accelerated Schools Resource Guide.* San Francisco: Jossey-Bass Inc., 1993.

Johnson, Susan. *Teachers at Work.* Basic Books, 1990.

Kotter, John. *Leading Change.* Boston: Harvard Business School Press, 1996.

Kozol, Johnathan. *Savage Inequalities.* New York: Crown Publishers, 1991.

Sources Consulted

Merriam-Webster Dictionary. Springfield: Merriam-Webster, Incorporated, 1997.

Monroe, Lorraine. *Nothing's Impossible.* New York: Public Affairs, 1997.

Orfield, Gary, Susan Eaton and the Harvard Project on School Desegregation. *Dismantling Desegregation: the Quiet Reversal of Brown v. Board of Education.* New York: The New Press, 1996.

Ploski, Harry and James Williams. *Reference Library of Black America*, Volume II. New York: Gale Research, Inc., 1990. p. 344.

Ploski, Harry and James Williams. *Reference Library of Black America*, Volume V. New York: Gale Research, Inc., 1990. p. 1389

Rioux, William and Nancy Berla. *Innovations In Parent & Family Involvement.* Princeton Junction, New Jersey: Eye On Education, 1993.

Sax, Gilbert. *Principles of Educational Measurement and Evaluations.* Belmont: Wadsworth Publishing, 1974.

Schlechty, Phillip. *Schools For the Twenty-first Century.* San Francisco: Jossey-Bass Publishers, 1990.

Stainback, Susan and William Stainback. *Curriculum Considerations in Inclusive Classrooms.* Baltimore: Paul H. Brookes Publishing, 1992.

Tucker, Marc and Judy Codding. *Standards for Our Schools.* San Francisco: Jossey-Bass Publishers, 1998.

United States Department of Education. *Turning Around Low Performing Schools.* Washington, D.C.: United States Department of Education, 1998.

Vassquez, Rosetta. *Reforming Chicago Schools: The Intended and Unintended Consequences.* DeKalb, IL: LEPS Press, 1994.

Wiggins, Grant. *Assessing Student Performance.* San Francisco: Jossey-Bass Publishers, 1993.

Wise, Arthur. *Rich Schools, Poor Schools, The Promise of Equal Educational Opportunity.* Chicago: The University of Chicago Press, 1972.

Magazines and Journals

P. Black and D. William. "Inside the black box: Raising standards through classroom assessment." *Phi Delta Kappan* Vol. 80, No. 2: 139-148, 1998.

T. Corcoran and M. Goertz. "Instructional capacity and high performance." *Educational Researcher* Vol. 24. No 9: 27-31, 1995.

Reports

"Annual Report of the Superintendent of Common Schools of the State of New York." New York State Assembly, 1845.

"Building on the Best, Learning from What Works: Six Promising Schoolwide Reform Programs." American Federation of Teachers, 1998.

"Forty Developmental Assets for Elementary Students." Minnesota: Search Institute, 2004.

Goals 2000. Washington, DC.: National Education Goals Panel, 1994.

Improving Low-Performing High Schools. American Federation of Teachers, 1999.

Sources Consulted

Michigan Department of Education. *Description Michigan's AYP Formula.* 2002.

National Commission on Excellence. "A Nation at Risk." 1981.

National Education Association. "Modernizing Our Schools: What Will it Cost?" 2000.

Rothstein, Richard. "What Do We Know About Declining (or Rising) Student Achievement?" Arlington, VA: Educational Research Service and American Association of School Administrators, 1997.

Newspapers

Education Week. "Studies Find Benefits from 'America's Choice.'" April 21, 2004.

INDEX

Index